West Academic
Emeritus Advisory Board

West Academic Publishing's Law School Advisory Board

The Rule

The Little Book on Perpetuities

Second Edition

Donald H. Gjerdingen
Professor of Law
Indiana University Maurer School of Law

A SHORT & HAPPY GUIDE® SERIES

WEST
ACADEMIC
PUBLISHING

a short & happy guide series is a trademark registered in the U.S. Patent and Trademark Office.

© 2017 LEG, Inc. d/b/a West Academic
© 2021 LEG, Inc. d/b/a West Academic
    444 Cedar Street, Suite 700
    St. Paul, MN 55101
    1-877-888-1330

Printed in the United States of America

ISBN: 978-1-64708-514-8

To Kendra, Erick, and Kari, and to Eloise, Anette, and Lena—my beautiful lives in being.

Acknowledgments

I'm grateful to my colleague, Jeff Stake, for his comments and his enthusiasm for the subject. And to Ms. Mary Beth Boyer and Ms. Cassie Fitzwater for their careful work on the manuscript.

My thanks to Elizabeth Eisenhart, an editor who, when asked, "What about the Rule against Perpetuities?" did what so many generations of law students and lawyers have done—she laughed.

Bloomington, Indiana

June 2021

The Common-Law Rule Against Perpetuities

No interest is good unless it must vest, if at all, not later than twenty-one years after some life in being at the creation of the interest.

—John Chipman Gray, The Rule Against Perpetuities
§ 201, at 191 (4th ed. 1942)

Table of Contents

PART 3. HOW THE RULE CAME TO BE

PART 6. THE FUTURE & POLICIES OF THE RULE

Chapter 18. Congress, Taxes, & Abolition of the Rule— the Humpty-Dumpty World of Modern Perpetuities

PART 7. A FINAL LOOK AT THE RULE

A Short & Happy Guide to The Rule

The Little Book on Perpetuities

Second Edition

The Rule against Perpetuities stands as an exotic Gordian-like weed in the common-law garden. Its roots lost in the dark and loamy politics of medieval England, its branches gnarled and deeply knotted, it lived for centuries of lawyers as a hardy nuisance, ever-by. Sharp and tendril-footed, it could draw blood from even the most careful of legal hands. And, in bloom, its touch could be fatal. Unlike anything else the soil of the common law has ever produced, it stands alone, a rule seemingly parched of human touch. All in all, it is a legal plant largely unloved.

—Student marginalia in a dusty casebook
in the Jerome Hall Law Library

Introduction

[L]et us not forget the bedeviled law student.

—Barton Leach, *Perpetuities in a Nutshell*,
51 Harv. L. Rev. 638, 638 (1938)

A. Law Students & the Rule Against Perpetuities

The Rule against Perpetuities is about grand fortunes and power, intrigue, politics, and lasting fame. It's also about big questions of property, families, and markets.

Why, then, do so many law students dread the Rule against Perpetuities? And how, too, did all this fun get lost in law school?

The problem is not with the students or the Rule, but how the story is told. Once dissected, the Rule is hardly as long-fanged as so many legal memories make it out to be.

B. Why We Study the Rule

Why do we study the Rule? In all, there are two good reasons. First, the Rule raises a wonderful policy question for the law: how far into the future may one generation control property? In one way

1

or another, every generation must answer it. For the last 350 years, the answer has been the Rule against Perpetuities.

Second, and most important, the Rule matters for practicing lawyers, especially those who draft wills and trusts. In the everyday practice of law, the Rule matters most for two big questions about wills and trusts:

- How many generations into the future may be favored by a gift?

- How long may gifts in trust last?

Both questions are important and practical. Both, too, matter in the lives of regular people. Here, the answer the Rule gives is *two generations.*

Thus, despite all the dark tales told about it, the Rule continues to play an important role in the legal garden.

C. How to Learn the Rule

Too often, the story of the Rule starts in the wrong place. Deep and complex definitions are thrown on a page. Then equation-like stories are told and strange answers given. Too often, it all reads like an owner's manual for a different math.

Done like this, as it is so often, the result is fabled confusion. Learning slows. Mystery remains. Even worse, it doesn't teach students what they need to know.

In truth, the Rule is eminently learnable. But the Rule's best learned by a different route. To learn the details of the Rule, you don't start with the details. You don't try to learn it, either, from inside its own world.

My starting point is this: there's a wonderful human story behind the Rule. It's rich and deep. It touches on families and markets, wealth and power. In truth, it has some of the best questions in law school.

Later, to be sure, some math-like logic was put in. But only because of the story lawyers decided to tell. Once you know the what the story is and who the characters are, all the details will follow. You'll remember the story, too, longer than the math.

D. Some Themes for This Book

In turn, here are some themes for this book. Many, too, are not what students expect.

- **The Rule Is Bigger (and More Fun) than You Think.** The Rule is center stage to a long-standing political battle in the common law. Ultimately, it's all about families versus markets as competing social arrangements for controlling property. The Rule, when it started, gave a much-needed answer.

- **The Rule Against Perpetuities Is Not Like Other Rules.** This Rule is not like other rules of the common law. It's different, and in many ways. So is how it's used and argued. It's not like anything else you'll learn in law school. It's unique in the law.

- **The Rule Changes How Lawyers Need to Think.** To learn the Rule, you have to stop thinking how lawyers usually think. It's that different. The Rule goes against "legal common sense." If you understand why, you've already learned much of the Rule.

- **The Rule Matters Most for Families & Estate Planning.** The Rule has big policy implications for a course in Property. But, in practice, the Rule matters most for families and estate planning. You can't practice wills and trusts without it. The Rule limits how far into the future gifts and beneficiaries can be.

- **Most Applications of the Rule Are Simple.** Casebooks often showcase strange or unusual applications of the Rule. In practice, though, the Rule's not exotic. The most common applications of the Rule, far and away, involve gifts to children and grandchildren, and sometimes great-grandchildren. Here, the workings of the Rule are clear. They're easy, too

- **There Are Diverse Policies Behind the Rule.** There are diverse (and engaging) policies behind the Rule. Some focus on alienability of property, but others are about justice between generations or family dynasties. Some policies have changed, slightly, over the last 350 years. But most still are the same.

- **The Rule Comes with a Politics.** A legal world with the Rule has very different politics than one without it. It's not a neutral rule. Among other things, the Rule curbs family dynasties and limits hereditary wealth. It also encourages markets and repurposing of property. If the Rule is repealed, those politics are limited.

E. Using This Book

Different people learn in different ways. Students come with different backgrounds, too. For some, it's all new. For others, it's a review.

Think of this book as a set of resources. You don't have to read through, cover to cover. All the pieces are here. It just depends what you want to learn first.

Whatever your background, though, it's probably best to read *A Modern Nutshell of the Rule* (Chapter 4) early on. It's an overview of this book. It also can be used later for review.

F. The Short & Happy Plan for This Book

Think of this book as a plan, in seven parts, to teach you everything you need to know about the Rule.

Part 1—An Approach to the Rule

Before looking at the Rule, it's important to know the why the Rule is bigger than you think, why it matters for the practice of law, and why it's different from other rules you study in law school.

Chapter 1—Why the Rule Matters for Law & Politics. The Rule matters most for daily matters of estate planning. But it also matters for big questions of property, families, dynasties, and wealth. It's not a small or unimportant rule. It matters as much now, too, as it did 350 years ago.

Chapter 2—Using the Rule—the Donative Gene & Future Generations. The Rule matters for donative gifts within the family, basically for wills and trusts. Once you know this, the Rule's emphasis of generations isn't so mysterious.

Chapter 3—Learning the Rule—Perpetuities & Legal Common Sense. If you understand why the Rule seems hard at first—it goes against legal common sense—you're already half done. Once done, you can quickly learn the other half.

Part 2—A Modern Nutshell of the Rule

Chapter 4—A Modern Nutshell of the Rule. An overview of the Rule and this book. The story of the Rule—and what you need to know—in a few pages. Think of it as an introduction, a study aid, and a summary.

Part 3—How the Rule Came to Be

How did the Rule come to be? It has a deep and wonderful history, full of big (and fun) questions. But the story rarely is told. Once you know it, though, you'll know the human reasons behind the Rule. You'll also know why we have it.

Chapter 5—Pieces of the Rule—Families vs. Markets. Ultimately, the Rule's at the center of a thousand-year-long debate in the common law. It's about how long families can control property and thus trump markets. Basically, it's families versus markets. It's about fee tails and fee simples, too.

Chapter 6—The Legal Setting of the Rule—Future Interests, Conditions, & Contingent Title. Within this larger debate, a particular legal setting invited the Rule. It involved future interests, conditions, and contingent title. This raised another issue: how long could families, by doing this, keep property in the family? This raised the specific setting for the Rule.

Chapter 7—The Family That Started It All—the *Duke of Norfolk's Case*. The Rule itself, which set how long families could use conditions, started with the *Duke of Norfolk's Case* in 1682. The case itself may be old, but story it tells isn't. It's a vivid and memorable story about families. Understand this one case and you'll understand most of the Rule. A bonus: it's about power, betrayal, and intrigue. It's filled with big personalities, too.

Chapter 8—How the *Duke of Norfolk's Case* Became a Special Rule. After the *Duke of Norfolk's Case*, the law could have developed in different ways. No one legal path was obvious. In the end, though, it ended up a rule unlike any other in the common law. It also created new ways for lawyers to argue. It's important to know why. This sets the stage for the full treatment of Gray's Rule.

Part 4—The Common-Law Rule of John Chipman Gray

Everything starts with John Chipman Gray's common-law Rule, even modern reforms. Here's what you'll learn:

Chapter 9—An Interlude—Personalities—John Chipman Gray. The Rule was written (and reformed) by strong personalities. Knowing a little about them can teach you a lot about the Rule. John Chipman Gray was the larger-than-life professor who drafted what is universally cited as the common-law Rule.

Chapter 10—Gray's Common-Law Rule—the Nutshell. This gives you an overview of the common-law Rule, what it requires, and how it works.

Chapter 11—The Cold Heart of Gray's Rule—Two Options & Some Rules of Thumb. The Rule is one of logical proof. It seems like math or geometry. This chapter explains the two—and only two—choices for every perpetuities problem. It also offers a proven way to solve them.

Chapter 12—Some Common Cases & Some Classic Traps. The Rule has many common applications, particularly for gifts to children or grandchildren. If you know these, you'll use them often. The Rule also is famous for classic traps. Most violations fall into one of six categories. If you know them, you'll avoid most drafting mistakes. This also highlights some special twists of the Rule.

Chapter 13—A Checklist, Some Problems, & Some Answers. This chapter offers a checklist for working through a perpetuities problem. It also provides some problems, with answers. Use them to test your progress. Once you're done, you'll know most of the Rule.

Chapter 14—A Perpetuities Miscellany—Some Advanced Topics. A few advanced topics for perpetuities. Charities, powers of appointment, class gifts, and saving clauses are covered. So are two related *how long* rules, the Rule against Accumulation of Trust Income, and the Rule against Suspension of the Power of Alienation.

Part 5—Modern Reform of the Common-Law Rule

Today, perpetuities law is mostly statutory. In turn, two reforms dominate modern perpetuities law—reformation and wait-and-see. If you know both, you'll understand any modern statute.

Chapter 15—An Interlude—Personalities—Barton Leach. The modern reform of the Rule starts with Professor Barton Leach. His ideas and energy inspired modern updates to the Rule.

Chapter 16—Reforms Generally—Reformation & Wait-and-See. Today, two modern reforms fix violations of the Rule—reformation and wait-and-see. This chapter explains the history and workings of each.

Chapter 17—The Age of Statutory Reform. The most widely adopted modern reform is the Uniform Statutory Rule Against Perpetuities (USRAP), first proposed in 1986. Another, and recent, reform is the two-generation standard offered by the *Restatement (Third) of Property*. Both use reformation and wait-and-see.

Part 6—The Future & Policies of the Rule

These are exciting times for the Rule. It's at the heart of big debates about taxes, social policy, and property. As lawyers, you'll decide the future of the Rule. And you'll get to debate some fun and exciting issues.

Chapter 18—Congress, Taxes, & Abolition of the Rule—the Humpty-Dumpty World of Modern Perpetuities. In the last two decades, some states have abolished the Rule. It's not a quarrel with the Rule itself, however. In grand American tradition, it's all about avoiding taxes. This *dynastic trust* movement plays a prominent role in the modern debate about perpetuities.

Chapter 19—A Few Big Ideas—Policies Behind the Rule. What justifies the Rule and its limits? What ultimate policies does it put in play? To debate the big issues, in class and in practice, you need to know. They're simple, fun, and compelling.

Part 7—A Final Look at the Rule

Chapter 20—What Would Nottingham Say? A final review of the Rule, its growth and use, and where it may go from here. What's the future of the Rule in American law? Most important, why the answer still matters for law today.

All in all, not so bad.

G. A Final & Not-So-Serious Note on Usage

When describing "the Rule" do you capitalize "against"? Is it the "Rule against Perpetuities" or the "Rule Against Perpetuities"? (Or is it even something else, like the "rule against perpetuities"?)

The good news: you can do whatever you want. If ever asked for authority, just cite Jesse Dukeminier, *Perpetuities: Contagious Capitalization*, 20 J. Legal Educ. 341 (1968).

The author is one of the great scholars of the Rule. And he needed 20 pages and 218 footnotes to say his piece. Tracing back through centuries of sources, he finds a classic use ("rule against perpetuities"), a modern use ("Rule against Perpetuities"), and a recent and suspect Bluebook use ("Rule Against Perpetuities").

It's a delightful read. An added bonus: it may be the narrowest law review topic ever.

I go with "Rule against Perpetuities." I think it's what he would have wanted.

PART 1

An Approach to the Rule

CHAPTER 1

Why the Rule Matters for Law & Politics

Property is full of antiquated rules drawn from the insular politics of some century long past. The Rule Against Perpetuities, however, is not one of them.

The Rule's a practical and oft-used rule in wills, trusts, and estate planning. That's reason enough. It matters for everyday lawyers.

What's often missed, though, is the larger role the Rule plays in law and politics. The Rule's part of a centuries-long intellectual and political debate. It's all about wealth, power, and families. That's never going away. And it still matters today.

Let's start with the practical first.

A. Practical Matters—Property & Future Interests

Law students often first meet the Rule in Property. There, it's presented as part of future interests. And here, too, is where it often gets lost.

The Rule's typically offered as a sub-rule of future interests. Its role, we're told, is one about the "remoteness of vesting."[1] Often, little more is said.

Done this way, though, much is lost. Here's why:

- **The Separate Maze of Future Interests.** Future interests are one thing, the Rule against Perpetuities is another. The two, of course, are related. But each has its own learning, too. Future interests is its own legal maze. It's hard learning, worth the effort. But in the hurry of learning future interests, the Rule's larger story often is left untold.

- **Future Interests & Trusts.** Today, virtually all future interests are in trusts. It's part of estate planning. As a result, first-year students often miss the dominant use of the Rule today.

- **Missing Questions of Property.** At its core, the Rule's about big questions of Property. Families, markets, and dynasties are not small things. Neither are opinions about them. Such questions belong in a Property course. Often, though, they get dropped.

Thus, as first encountered, much is missed about the Rule. It's hard for students to know, at first, why it matters.

B. Practical Matters—Wills & Trusts

Every course in Wills & Trusts covers the Rule. The reason: the Rule's applied daily in wills, trusts, and estate planning. That's its dominant application today.

---

[1] John Chipman Gray, The Rule Against Perpetuities x (4th ed. 1942) (preface to first edition).

Here, typically, is when most students face the Rule head-on. It's not a small part of the course either. Here's why:

- **The Common Law & Multiple Generations.** When it comes to donative transfers, the common law is special. Unlike other legal systems, it recognizes forms of multi-generational property. By using wills and trusts, donors can control property not just at death, but for several generations after.

- **The Legal Tools.** The legal tools used are future interests, trusts, and powers of appointment. Together, they allow donors to control future gifts.

- **The Role of the Rule.** In turn, the Rule limits how many future generations may be controlled. All three tools—future interests, trusts, and powers of appointment—are bound by the Rule.

The Rule matters most when drafting donative gifts within family:

- **Conditions in Gifts.** It controls how long, after death, donors can control property by using conditions in gifts of property.

- **Yet Unborn Beneficiaries.** It also controls what gifts, if any, can be given to "yet unborn" beneficiaries.

- **Private Trusts.** It determines how long private trusts can last.

Because of the Rule, the answer today is basically two generations. After that, donors can't control private gifts.

Here, too, is an interesting twist. In practice, violations of the Rule are rare. Why? It isn't because the Rule doesn't matter.

Instead, it's because practicing lawyers who do estate planning know the Rule. It's built into everything they do. It works.

C. Big Questions of Property—"Families vs. Markets"

Thus, the Rule has plenty of practical applications, but the Rule is more than that, too. It also matters for some significant and long-standing social questions about Property.

- **Families vs. Markets.** Writ large, the Rule's about "families vs. markets." How long should families, as families, be allowed to keep property in the family and thus off the market?

- **The Options.** Over the course of the common law, the answer has swung everywhere from "as long as the family continues" (i.e., fee tails) to "only one generation at time" (i.e., fee simples).

- **The Answer Today.** For the last 350 years, however, the answer has been "basically two generations." The legal reason: the Rule Against Perpetuities.

This debate, as we'll see, is at the very heart of the Rule, hiding in plain legal sight.

D. Big Political Questions, Big Political Values

The Rule, too, is part of a larger intellectual and political debate. It's all about wealth, power, and families.

The Rule also is central to a thousand-year-long debate in the common law. It's about baseline settings for political and social life.

Here's what's at stake:

- **Financial Nobility.** How many future generations can be guaranteed hereditary wealth? In short, how many generations of financial nobility are allowed?

- **Protection of Family Wealth.** How long can family wealth be protected from the creditors or follies of future family members?

- **Equal Protection Writ Large.** In America, is it fair that wealthy families (but not others) be allowed, by law, to guarantee yet unborn future generations a privileged financial future at birth? And, if so, for how many generations?

The answer to all these questions today is the Rule. And the Rule basically says "two generations" only.

These are big and fun questions. They're still relevant today.

CHAPTER 2

Using the Rule— the Donative Gene & Future Generations

Let's talk of graves, of worms, and epitaphs;
Make dust our paper and with rainy eyes
Write sorrow on the bosom of the earth,
Let's choose executors and talk of wills

—Richard II act 3, sc. 2

A. The Voice of Wills & Trusts

When people go to lawyers for estate planning, they come with two things. First, they come with lists of what they own. It may be homes, farms, businesses, pensions and personal accounts, or stocks and bonds. Second, they come with ideas about who gets that property when they die.

It wasn't always that way, of course. Before wills and trusts, people didn't have much say about property after they died. But wills and trusts changed all that. Empowered by wills, people now can speak at death and must be listened to. Empowered even more by trusts, people now can speak after death for a long time.

Thanks to wills and trusts, in short, the dead now can compete with the living for how property is used.

B. Future Hands & Voices

Once the dead are allowed to speak, the next question must be this: how deep into the future do their words bind? Just how long do solemn words at death matter?

Here, making future plans for family is what people do. People first think of family they know and will leave behind—spouses and partners, sons and daughters, and grandchildren and friends.

And here, too, they may ask what Shakespeare's "seeds of time"[1] may hold. What will children and grandchildren do? What will life hold for them? Will they have good lives? Will they marry? What help might they need?

They may think of deeper generations, too. They may think of children yet unborn and lives yet unlived. What will my great-grandchildren be like? What will their names and passions be? Even if I never get to hold them or see their faces, can I still help them?

C. Estate Plans & Contingencies

Filled with such thoughts, people will come to you and ask for an estate plan. Some may need wills or revocable trusts. Others may need irrevocable trusts, class gifts, or powers of appointment. Some may need them all.

In the process, talk will turn to contingencies. What about failed marriages, unexpected deaths, or spouses left behind? What about gifts to grandchildren at 21 or 35? What, too, about great-

---

[1] William Shakespeare, The Tragedy of Macbeth act 1, sc. 3 ("If you can look into the seeds of time and say which grain will grow and which will not, speak then to me.").

grandchildren, or after? And, if clients have enough money, what about dynasties or far-off inherited wealth?

D. Contingencies & Perpetuities

Right here—just at this point—is where the Rule against Perpetuities matters. When people ask about such things, you must tell them this: you can help the people you love for only so long— *two generations.*

After two generations, nothing more can be done. After that, those future lives are on their own. After the perpetuities period ends, your voice no longer matters.

For this reason, the Rule raises a classic question about social wealth and power: if a family has enough wealth, can they guarantee support and protection for distant generations? If they want, can they free descendants, known and unknown, from common birth?

Here, the common-law Rule against Perpetuities gives them a clear answer: you only get two generations. After that, your family must be on its own. You can't protect them. They can be spendthrifts or savers, fools or geniuses. It's all up to them.

For clients and lawyers, therefore, the Rule gives this advice: don't worry about contingencies too far in the future. You may want great-grandchildren yet unborn as beneficiaries of a trust, but the law may not allow it. The law, you must accept, sets some things off as too remote. Here, the law doesn't allow you a legal worry.

E. Doing Perpetuities Right

Today, with reforms, violations of the Rule no longer are fatal. Reformation and wait-and-see can cure mistakes. And, as such, challenges are few.

But modern reforms are no reason to avoid learning the classic common-law Rule. Mistakes—even if later fixed—still cost in time and trouble. If you know the common-law Rule and do it right the first time, you'll never need reforms to save your work.

Even with reforms, therefore, the common-law Rule still matters. If done right the first time, here's what you get:

- **Quick Answers.** Apply the Rule as you draft the document. If you do, you'll know instantly whether you've done it right.

- **Certainty.** Here, the law is black and white. Either the contingency's valid or it's not. There is no doubt and there is no gray.

- **Ease of Proof.** The answer comes as mathematical proof. No policies to argue or facts to find. No pleadings or depositions, either. Everything can be done, at your desk, in seconds.

This is why knowing the common-law Rule is so important. If you know the Rule, you'll give clients right answers and do work right the first time. If you do, three good things will happen:

- You'll comply with the Rule.

- Your client's gifts will happen.

- Your work and your client's plan will be protected from attack.

F. Other Matters of Practice

This, of course, is just the start. As we'll later see:

- The Rule governs all kinds of gifts within the family, especially those to children and grandchildren.[2]

---

[2] See Chapter 12.

- The Rule applies to trusts and, among other things, determines how long private trusts can last.[3]

- It also applies to other matters of estate planning like class gifts, powers of appointment, and some gifts to charities.[4]

But, for now, this much should be clear: the Rule against Perpetuities matters to practicing lawyers. It's far from an unused rule.

---

[3]   See Chapter 19.
[4]   See Chapter 14.

CHAPTER 3

Learning the Rule— Perpetuities & Legal Common Sense

There is something in the subject which seems to facilitate error. Perhaps it is because the mode of reasoning is unlike that with which lawyers are most familiar.

—John Chipman Gray, The Rule Against
Perpetuities xi (4th ed. 1942)

A. The Rule & Legal Common Sense

The reputation of the Rule against Perpetuities, whispered in the stacks, is fabled. If student rumors are believed, it's some impenetrable legal mystery. No one life is long enough to learn it. Better, the whispers continue, to live in a world without it.

Why is this so? Why, of all the rules in law school, does this Rule seem so hard? Why does this particular rule, of all the rules you learn, seem so much harder than you think it should be?

It's not, I can guarantee, because the idea behind the Rule is hard. It's not because the learning of it has to be hard, either.

Instead, the answer is simple: the Rule runs counter to legal common sense. How the Rule works, on the inside, is not how lawyers normally are trained to think. You can't approach it like other legal rules. Instead, you need to learn something new.

If you understand this one point, you'll already understand much of the Rule.

What is legal common sense? All law students learn it. But they don't always know they are learning it. Legal common sense simply means the usual, expected assumptions behind legal analysis. For example, here are four points students learn early and often in law school:

- **Facts Matter.** Lawyers care about *facts*. Law turns on what did happen, not what might have happened. Real cases depend on real facts, not hypothetical ones. Start with the facts and know them cold. Sort the true from the false, then use only the true. Don't speculate. If you worry about questions not reasonably raised by the facts, you lose, especially on exams.

- **Concentrate on Probable or Likely Events.** Law cares about what's probable or likely. Contracts are drafted that way. So are deeds, wills, and plea agreements. In Torts, negligence looks to probabilities (so says Learned Hand) and to foreseeable injuries and plaintiffs. The same idea moves throughout the law, from contracts and crimes to antitrust and tax.

- **Custom, Expectations, and Efficiency Matter.** Custom is the heart of the common law. Settled expectations matter. Lawyers care about usual expectations or what reasonable people would do.

At the same time, good lawyers don't ask unnecessary questions. Some events are so unlikely even the most careful of lawyers wouldn't worry. And certainly, if something is impossible—if it just can't happen—it can be ignored.

- **Important People Are Named in Legal Documents.** Contracts name parties. So do deeds, complaints, and wills. In a well-drafted document, everything is clear, organized, indexed, and tabbed. Important people always are named. If you're not named, you're not part of the deal, contract, or agreement.

These assumptions are so common and fundamental they go without saying in law school. Students don't discuss or debate them. Instead, they just use them, over and over, day after day. After long months of this—done every day in every class—it hardens into legal reflex. It becomes legal common sense. It's just how lawyers think.

Until, of course, law students meet the Rule against Perpetuities.

B. Legal Common Sense Meets Something Else: The Rule Against Perpetuities

When students first see *Rule against Perpetuities* on the syllabus, they assume it's just one more rule to learn, like so many before. Students already learned the *mailbox rule* in Contracts and the *eggshell skull rule* in Torts. They assume, quite reasonably, this new rule is just like the others.

But it's not. And that's the problem. The Rule against Perpetuities isn't like the others. In truth, it's unlike any other rule you learn in law school. But students aren't told this. And, quite reasonably, they have no reason to think otherwise.

The first day students meet the Rule against Perpetuities, therefore, they use legal common sense, exactly as they were trained. Students think about probable events and look for real facts, just as they were trained. But it doesn't work. And there's confusion.

C. The Strange Land of Perpetuities

Then things get worse. In the Land of Perpetuities, legal common sense isn't just unhelpful, it's *wrong*.

Here, everything is opposite: real facts and what happens in the real world are ignored, while hypotheticals and what's remote or even what's impossible are made central. Here, what was good is now bad, and what was bad is now good.

In the Land of the Rule against Perpetuities, here's a sampling of new legal truths:

- What matters is *what might happen*. What actually did happen later doesn't matter. Even if some remote event didn't happen afterwards, assume it still could have happened.

- The Rule may strike down an interest based on facts known to be false. Here, the Rule assumes an 80-year-old woman can give birth even when everyone in the world, including her, knows she can't.

- The Rule may strike down an interest based on *hypothetical* facts so remote or unlikely, no careful lawyer would otherwise worry about them. But the standard for the Rule isn't whether something is likely or probable. Instead, it's whether there's any mathematical possibility, *however remote*. One chance in a billion is enough to strike an interest down.

- A person needed to validate an interest under the Rule, a *measuring life*, need not be named in the instrument. In fact, it may not be obvious at first who the measuring life is.

In the Land of Perpetuities, in short, what's wrong is common sense itself. Here, the Rule *punishes* lawyers for using it. Once you enter the domain of the Rule, using legal common sense could be malpractice.

D. Knowing the First Half of the Rule

This, in a nutshell, is why the Rule, at first, seems harder than it is. Students are trained, day after day, to think one way and then—without notice—they're punished for using what they learned. This is cruel psychology. If you know this from the start, however, you'll avoid confusion and mistakes.

You'll see similar quirks of thinking in other aspects of the Rule, too. This is not the end of the list. Among other things, you'll see how the shape of the Rule is different from other common-law rules. Plus, the arguments lawyers need to make are different, too.[1]

The lesson: be prepared to learn something new. Understand, too, what your normal legal reflexes are. And try not to use them.

---

[1]   See Chapters 8, 10-12.

A Modern Nutshell of the Rule

A Modern Nutshell of the Rule

The Rule against Perpetuities is famous for nutshells.[1] What, in a few pages, is it all about? And what are the key points, big and small, students need to know?

A. The Larger Role It Plays in Law & Politics[2]

Most students think the Rule against Perpetuities is narrow and arcane, at best a legal curiosity. And, perhaps, too, something from a different legal age, now long past.

But it's not.

In truth, the Rule plays a big role in law, politics, and society. It matters both for Property and for Wills & Trusts. And it still matters very much today.

---

[1] See W. Barton Leach, *Perpetuities in a Nutshell*, 51 Harv. L. Rev. 638 (1938).
[2] Chapter 1.

The Rule raises wonderful big questions:

- **Gifts to Those Unborn.** Can gifts be given to people yet unborn? What about future grandchildren or great-grandchildren, yet to be conceived?

- **Families vs. Markets.** Should property always be alienable? Or can donors limit alienability to keep property in the family? If so, for how long?

- **Family Dynasties.** Should law support family dynasties in property? And, if so, for how long?

- **Hereditary Wealth.** Would it be right (or good), in America, to allow some form of hereditary wealth? And, if so, for how long?

- **Financial Nobility.** Should law allow a fee tail in modern property like stocks and bonds and give blessing to financial nobility?

Understanding how all these pieces, both big and small, fit together is part of a good legal education, too.

B. Why the Rule Matters for Practicing Lawyers[3]

The Rule raises big political and social questions for Property. That's why it's part of that course.

But the typical application of the Rule today is estate planning. Overwhelmingly, the Rule matters for families. It matters, daily, for drafting trusts. It also matters for wills.

It's far from an unused rule, too. It sets basic rules about gifts to children, grandchildren, and other relatives. But it matters for gifts to strangers, too.

---

[3]   Chapters 2 & 12.

In particular, it limits how far into the future beneficiaries can be. Giving gifts outright to living people is easy. But if donors look too far into the future, the Rule may apply.

Here are two settings, always worrisome:

- **Gifts to Future Descendants, as yet Unborn.** Often, this is grandchildren. But it could be great-grandchildren or others, too.

- **Gifts with Conditions.** Basically, if property goes one way if some future event happens, but another if it doesn't.

These are not unusual requests. When the questions come, you must tell clients if such gifts are allowed or not. To give them the right answer, you must know the Rule.

C. Why This Rule Is Different[4]

The Rule against Perpetuities isn't like any other rule you learn in law school. You need to know why it's different. This is a simple point. But it's rarely talked about.

What makes the Rule different? Here's a start:

- **Another Type of Rule.** This Rule is not like other common-law rules. The Rule doesn't have defenses, exceptions, or counter-rules. There is no back-and-forth. There is no borderline, either, and there is no gray. It's just "yes" or "no."

- **How Lawyers Think.** Unlike other legal questions, you won't read for facts and issues. Instead, you'll look forward and ask which of two hypotheticals apply. That's it.

---

[4] Chapters 2, 8, 10 & 11.

- **How Lawyers Argue.** For the Rule, the arguments for lawyers are different, too. You don't argue about cases, policies, or facts. Instead, you battle with "logical proofs." If done right, both sides get the same answer, too.

- **Against Legal Common Sense.** Nothing you've learned before in law school will help you learn the Rule. Why? The Rule has a different logic. Here, all lawyers must be taught anew. To learn the Rule, you must stop thinking how lawyers normally do.

D. How Did the Rule Come to Be?[5]

What gave rise to the Rule against Perpetuities all started out, centuries ago, as a drawn-out political battle between families and markets. It went back and forth.

Here's the progression:

- **"Families Forever"—Fee Tails (1285).** The fee tail kept property in the family as long as the family existed. In turn, markets did not apply. Once in the family, property was inalienable. This kept land off the market. It also preserved family wealth.

- **Then "Markets Forever"—Fee Simples (1472).** In response, some 200 years later, common law courts— by the device of "docking the entail"—allowed occupants to change fee tails into fee simples. This brought back markets. As a result, families could not, by law, control property for more than a single generation.

---

[5] Chapters 5 & 6.

- **Then Countermove by Families-Future Interests &
  Conditions ("Families for a While") (1472-1682).**
  In response, wealthy families (and their lawyers)
  created future interests. This allowed families to
  control property for multiple generations. While less
  than what fee tails allowed, this was more than pure
  markets allowed.

Now, we get to a particular problem that, ultimately, gave rise
to the Rule:

- **Future Interests, Conditions, & Multiple Futures.**
  To help with estate planning, donors started to put
  conditions in future interests. This lets donors plan
  for different futures. If the condition was met,
  property went one way. But, if not, it went another.

- **Unresolved Conditions & Contingent Title.** While
  the conditions were unresolved, however, ultimate
  title was contingent. As a result, property was tied
  up.

- **Unresolved Conditions & Families.** During the same
  time, the property also stayed in the family.

Thus, the critical question came down to this: "How long"
should contingent title be allowed to exist?

- **Families vs. Markets.** Some allowance for families
  seemed reasonable. But if it was too long, markets
  would be limited. So would the social and economic
  benefits of markets.

- **The Ghost of the Fee Tail.** There was another
  concern, too. The longer the contingency went on,
  the longer the property stayed in the family and off
  the market. This raised another problem: whatever

time allowed families, it couldn't be too close to the fee tail. Why? That would be a "perpetuity."

Thus, the question was this: "How long" could conditions in future interests remain unresolved for the benefit of families?

E. The Start of the Rule—the *Duke of Norfolk's Case*—Lives in Being[6]

The answer—which becomes the Rule against Perpetuities—starts with the *Duke of Norfolk's Case* (1682), some 350 years ago.

The Nature of the Case. The case, of course, involved future interests and conditions. A father was worried about the fate of his sons after his death.

As drafted, future title turned on whether his first son died without heirs while his second son was still alive. If the first son did, property went one way. If he didn't, it went another.

The question: Was this "too long" to wait? We wouldn't know the answer until his first son's life played out. As a practical matter, that likely would be decades after the father's death.

The judge in the case, Lord Nottingham, gave a famous answer. And it started the Rule against Perpetuities.

The "Compass of a Life." Nottingham's famous measure: the contingency would be resolved within the life of the eldest son. It would happen, he said, within "the compass of a life." Thus, the contingency was not too long. It was not a perpetuity.

The lesson was this: if we need to wait, after your death, to see what happens to your children, that's fine. That's not too long. We'll give that to families.

---

[6]   Chapter 7.

Contingencies & "Lives in Being." Here, too, was a big lesson. "How long" for families wouldn't be measured at first by months or years, but by human lives.

This measure became "lives in being." The lives didn't have to be your children (although it often was). It could be any person then alive.

Nottingham's Rule. Thus, Nottingham's first version of the Rule was this: if you knew the person—if the contingency would be resolved by a person then alive—it was valid. And that's an easy rule. It's not hard to apply. There's nothing scary about it.

The good news: Nottingham's Rule still is valid today. The problem: courts didn't leave Nottingham's Rule alone. Instead, they added more.

F. Those Extra 21 Years[7]

Beyond Nottingham's Rule. Over the next 150 years, step-by-step, courts went beyond "lives in being." Eventually, they added an extra 21 years to the period. Finally, "how long" became firmly fixed at "lives in being plus 21 years."

Future Lives. The extra 21 years added a twist to the Rule: by going beyond "the compass of a life," beneficiaries now could include people "yet-to-be-born." Contingencies now, in some ways, could cover future lives.

Complications. Those extra 21 years, however, made the Rule more complex. The reason: "21 years" didn't track how people thought about generations. As a result, it made the Rule easier to violate.

---

[7]   Chapters 10, 12 & 17.

G. The Famous Common-Law Rule of John Chipman Gray[8]

In the 200 years after the *Duke of Norfolk's Case*, the Rule gained dozens of twists and fine points. It also had its own disputes. People even argued what "the Rule" really was.

One Person, One Book. Finally, in 1886, the common-law Rule found a permanent home. It also found a single voice. The Rule was trimmed and codified by John Chipman Gray in his book, *The Rule Against Perpetuities*.

After that, Gray and his book *become* the common-law Rule. In part, too, the Rule took on the formalistic jurisprudence of the times.

Gray's Rule. As drafted by Gray, the Rule became a single sentence:

No interest is good unless it might vest, if at all, not later than twenty-one years after some life in being at the creation of the interest.[9]

It's the same sentence, too, everywhere in the common-law world.

H. The Special Logic of Gray's Rule[10]

A defining feature of Gray's Rule was this: it used a math-like logic unlike any other thinking by lawyers. It also was stern, formalistic, and unforgiving.

Math-Like Logic. As applied, Gray's wasn't like the *mailbox rule* in Contracts or the *eggshell skull rule* in Torts. Instead, it

---

[8]   Chapters 9 & 10.

[9]   John Chipman Gray, The Rule Against Perpetuities § 201, at 191 (4th ed. 1942).

[10]   Chapters 10 & 11.

worked like a theorem for math or geometry.[11] Here's how it worked:

- **Logical Proofs.** If asked if a gift complies with the Rule, you can't just say "yes" or "no." Facts aren't argued, either. Instead, you must "prove" your answer by a certain logic.

- **The Manner of Proofs.** In turn, there are different proofs, one for "yes" and one for "no." Each proof, too, has a different style.

- **The Proof for Complying with the Rule—Naming Measuring Lives.** To prove a contingency complies with the Rule, you must show the contingency will, as a matter of logic, "happen or not" within 21 years of a life in being.

- **The Proof for a Violation of the Rule—Telling Stories.** To prove a violation, you need only show a contingency "might not" be resolved within the perpetuities period. A single possibility is enough. Actual probabilities do not matter, either. The method: you tell hypothetical stories, often with uncommon and unusual assumptions, about what "might happen" looking forward.

Two Legal Boxes. Thus, under the Rule, there always are two different legal boxes. One is proof the contingency complies with the Rule. The other is proof it doesn't. It's always one or the other. They're mutually exclusive.

---

[11] As a student once said to me, "It was as if Euclid and his geometry theorems had gone to law school."

Picking the Right Box. Once you pick the right box, it's easy to do the proof. The key skill: knowing which box (and proof) to try. The right answer is always the same.

Against Legal Common Sense. Lawyers, of course, don't think like this. It's not how they're trained. Even more, the logic of the Rule often is exactly *opposite* of how lawyers are taught to think. In many ways, it violates legal common sense.

Fatal Errors & No Fixes. Gray's Rule was strict and unforgiving. Any mistake was fatal. If an error was made, the contingency was struck down. Even worse, mistakes could not be fixed. There were no second chances.

I. Practical Applications of the Rule[12]

From the beginning, the goal of the Rule was to set boundaries for drafting family gifts in wills and trusts. That's still, far and away, its main use.

Because of that, it's important to know how the Rule operates for typical estates. This is how it will play out, day after day, for most families.

Wills & Revocable Trusts. In practice, the most widely-used documents are wills and revocable trusts. In that setting, here's how the Rule typically works:

- Any condition can be used for a donor's children.

- Any condition, as well, can be used for named living grandchildren (or any other named living person).

- But gifts to "yet-to-be-born" grandchildren are limited to reaching the age of 21.

---

[12] Chapter 12.

- No other "yet-to-be-born" later generations can be covered.

Irrevocable Trusts. Less frequently, irrevocable trusts may be used, too. Here, though, gifts are even more restricted. Now, everything moves up a generation:

- Any condition can be used for named living children and grandchildren.

- But gifts to "yet-to-be-born" children are limited to reaching the age of 21.

- Gifts to "yet-to-be-born" grandchildren (and any other later "yet-to-be born" generations) are invalid.

General Use in Practice. Given the origin of the Rule in the *Duke of Norfolk's Case*, it shouldn't surprise how the Rule generally applies to donative gifts in wills and trusts. Here's how it works:

- It mostly covers "lives in being."

- It has limited application to beneficiaries as yet unborn.

- It favors direct descendants over others.

J. Classic Traps & Barton Leach's Characters[13]

Along with the Rule came classic mistakes or errors. Often, violations turned on assumptions or logic used nowhere else in the law. Because of that, even good and careful lawyers might unwittingly violate the Rule.

Typically, too, errors fell into set categories. They tended, again and again, to be of certain kinds. That alone was reason to know them.

---

[13] Chapter 12.

For law students, the classic traps are always special lessons. The reason: Professor Barton Leach, a famous perpetuities scholar, gave some of them special names. They included such fanciful legal creatures as the Fertile Octogenarian, the Unborn Widow, and the Slothful Executor, among others.

Today, Leach's characters are part of perpetuities lore. They're part of every casebook, too. They not only became famous reminders for drafting, but they also spurred modern reform.

The lesson for law students: know them and enjoy them.

K. Modern Reform of the Rule—Uniform Statutory Rule Against Perpetuities (USRAP) + Restatement (Third) of Property[14]

Over the last 35 years, however, there's been significant statutory reform of the common-law Rule.

Uniform Statutory Rule Against Perpetuities (USRAP). Of these, the most important is the Uniform Statutory Rule Against Perpetuities (USRAP), first proposed in 1986. It's the most widely adopted reform today.

The Workings of USRAP—Gray's Rule + Fixing Mistakes. In operation, here's how USRAP works:

- USRAP starts with Gray's Rule. It doesn't try to change it. If a gift complies with the Rule, nothing more is needed.

- If a mistake is made, however, USRAP doesn't strike down the contingency (as Gray would have done). Instead, it allows mistakes to be fixed.

---

[14] Chapters 15, 16 & 17.

- The goal of USRAP: make compliance with the Rule universal.

How Mistakes are Fixed—"Wait-and-See" & Reformation. USRAP fixes mistakes in two ways:

- **Wait-and-See.** This is a remedy special to perpetuities. It means waiting to see, by actual later events, whether contingencies are resolved.

- **Reformation.** Then, if not, USRAP allows reformation to fix the mistake. This involves asking a court to change the contingency to comply with the Rule.

Restatement (Third) of Property. Another important modern reform is the *Restatement (Third) of Property*. This takes a simple, yet comprehensive approach:

- Rather than starting with Gray's Rule, it offers an alternative Rule.

- Instead of using the traditional "lives in being plus 21 years," it extends the period to two full generations.

- This makes the Rule much easier to apply. It also eliminates many of the classic traps.

- It then uses reformation to fix any mistakes.

A Perpetuities Peace. By fixing mistakes, modern reforms offer a perpetuities peace. Malpractice actions are limited. So are attacks on wills and trusts by dissatisfied relatives. Most important, modern reforms let the Rule and its policies work.

L. Recent Repeal of the Rule & the Return of the Fee Tail[15]

In recent years, some states have abolished the Rule. Others have significantly extended the period to as long as 500 or 1000 years.

Not About Merits of the Rule. Significantly, however, it has nothing to do with the merits of the Rule itself. Why, then, was it done? It was all about avoiding taxes.

Federal Estate Taxes & Tax Havens. In this case, states repealed the Rule so wealthy clients, if they moved assets to the state, could avoid federal estate taxes. It was about creating tax havens. It also was about attracting the trust assets and management fees that came with it.

Dynastic Trust Movement. With significant extension or repeal of the Rule, clients now can set up long-term family trusts. In contrast to the common law, this allows creation of "dynastic trusts."

Problems With Dynastic Trusts. The dynastic trust movement, though, remains controversial:

- **Return of the Fee Tail.** The repeal of the Rule allows fee tails in trusts. It brings back, much like the original fee tail, family dynasties in property.

- **Endorsement of Long-Term Hereditary Wealth.** For the first time in American history, this allows creation of long-term family and hereditary wealth in trusts.

---

[15] Chapter 18.

M. The Deeper Politics & Place of the Rule[16]

The Rule first was created, centuries ago, to deal with families and future interests. But it's taken on a broader legal and social role since. Today, it's embedded in other doctrine, too. There is, to be sure, a deeper politics to it.

If asked, "What would happen if the Rule goes away?" here's what we could say.

1. Contingent Title in Real Property. The first application of the Rule was contingent title in real property. To some extent, that's been moderated today:

- Most wealth consists of personal property (e.g., stock, bonds, and mutual funds).

- Future interests today exist almost exclusively in trusts. This allows a trustee to buy and sell property in the trust.

At the same time, even in trust, property still is tied up. The wealth stays in the family. And full markets can't yet apply.

Without the Rule, a permanent trust could protect family wealth forever. It's a return of the fee tail. That's what happened with dynastic trusts.

2. Justice Between Generations. The Rule also serves as a practical working bargain between generations. It measures, in generations, how far into the future a donor may control property. In turn, it's also how many generations past the present generation must respect.

Here, the Rule's "two generation" measure seems about right. In practice, two generations means children and grandchildren.

---

[16] Chapter 19.

That's what most donors live to see. Thus, in a general way, the Rule limits control to people who knew each other face-to-face.

Without the Rule, control could go generations deeper. Then, it would be strangers controlling strangers.

3.　**The Equipoise of Trusts.** The Rule and trusts go together. The Rule determines how long private trusts can last. In practice, the "two generations" of the Rule limits the number of trust beneficiaries. It also facilitates repurposing of property. Repealing the Rule thus unravels the role and balance of trusts. Private trusts "forever" are not part of the common law.

4.　**Limits on Hereditary Wealth.** This is the big one. The Rule limits how long hereditary wealth, by law, can last. Because of the Rule, family wealth must, in essence, be repurposed every two generations. Then, once done, each generation is on its own, for good or bad.

If the Rule is repealed, however, all that changes:

- Fee tails would be allowed in trusts.

- So would long-term family dynasties.

- Future generations, even distant ones, could be guaranteed wealth at birth.

Repeal of the Rule, quite simply, allows the creation of financial nobility.

N.　The Future of the Rule[17]

Today, with reforms, the Rule can be applied without destroying property. Because mistakes can be fixed, it also can be more easily applied.

---

[17]　Chapter 20.

The repeal of the Rule, in some states, has brought back the fee tail. It also brings new controversy about limits, if any, on hereditary wealth.

This brings with it the need to talk, even more, about the Rule. These are exciting times for the Rule. They're also important for law students who know the Rule, how it came about, and what it does.

All in all, the Rule still plays an important social and legal role today. It started 350 years ago as a Rule about families and markets, dynasties and wealth. And it still is.

PART 3

How the Rule
Came to Be

CHAPTER 5

Pieces of the Rule— "Families vs. Markets"

Why do we have the Rule? What role did it play in the common law? How did it come to be?

Soon we'll look at the Rule itself. But first you'll need to know the larger social and legal setting that gave rise to the Rule.

The big picture is this: to understand future interests and the Rule against Perpetuities, first you must understand what our legal world was like without them.

In a world without future interests, what could families do? What options existed for donative gifts? What role, too, did markets (or the lack of them) play?

The questions here are these:

- **Families vs. Markets.** Why is there a tension, deep in the common law, between the common goals of families and the workings of markets?

- **No Role for the Rule.** In a world of only fee tails or fee simples, why is there no need for the Rule?

- **Families & Fee Simples.** After the common law ended fee tails and moved to fee simples, what was missing for families?

So let's see, writ large, what the tale of the Rule is and how it came to be.

That's next.

A. The Big Context—Families vs. Markets

The Rule against Perpetuities is part of a larger debate about political and social power. It all turned on dividing control of property between families and markets:

- **Families vs. Markets.** Writ large, the Rule's about "families vs. markets." How long should families, as families, be allowed to keep property in the family (and thus off the market)?

- **The Legal Options.** Over the course of the common law, the answer has swung everywhere from "as long as the family continues" (i.e., fee tails) to "only one generation at a time" (i.e., fee simples).

- **The Answer Today.** For the last 350 years, however, the answer has been "basically two generations." The legal reason: the Rule Against Perpetuities.

Simple enough, isn't it?

Now, let's look at the particular pieces. And, after that, how the Rule itself got written.

B. The Pieces—the Fee Tail ("Families Forever")

The Rule's fundamentally about an oh-so-human tension between families and markets.

The starting point here is the fee tail. And the fee tail, of course, is all about families.

- **"Families Forever."** First allowed by statute in 1285, the fee tail let families keep land in the family forever (so long as generations continued). It was, in essence, a series of life estates. Each new generation, again and again, got occupancy for life. In effect, the property (and wealth) was "owned" by the family itself.

- **The Beneficiaries & Politics of Fee Tails.** Of course, fee tails (as intended) helped the nobility. Wealth stayed in the same families. At the same time, fee tails limited social mobility for others.

- **"Markets Do Not Apply."** Significantly, fee tails and markets were mutually exclusive. The fee tail kept property off the market. Property bound by a fee tail was inalienable. Family members could not sell their interest. Creditors could not reach the property, either. This also protected family wealth.

Here, families dominate markets. Plus, the status quo dominates change.

C. The Pieces—the Fee Simple ("Markets Forever")

Now comes a political counter-move. While fee tails favored families and existing social power, they also raised broader economic and social concerns:

- Life tenants had little incentive to make improvements since they couldn't capture any value they added.

- Keeping property off the market limited overall social wealth because property couldn't be put to its highest and best economic use.

- It kept social life stratified and inhibited social change.

Docking the Entail. Thus, some 200 years later, common-law judges ended the fee tail. By a bit of legal conjuring (called docking the entail), the judges let markets apply. Now, just for the asking, tenants could turn fee tails into fee simples. And, of course, they did.

"Markets Forever." In turn, the fee simple became the dominant form of ownership. Fee simples always were alienable. Markets could apply any time.

The Beneficiaries & Politics of Markets. Once fee tails became fee simples, owners had more options. They had full choice on how to use the property. They could develop it, sell it, or give it away. In turn, markets also loosened existing social and political ties. The world, in all kinds of ways, was more fluid.

D. A Possible Carveout for Families in a Fee Simple World?

Now, we reach a critical stage in the social story that will give us the Rule. Let's be clear what it is:

- **Markets Are Staying.** At this point, markets and fee simples are part of an increasingly modern world. There's no turning back. That's understood.

- **Fee Tails Are Gone Forever.** No one is asking for fee tails to come back. Those are gone forever. That's understood, too.

But now, too, there seemed a gap. And it was about families.

The fee tail had its faults. But, at core, it was about families. And it had a resonating human quality. It was about parents helping and protecting later generations. It was about using property to keep a family together, too.

Thus, the question now was this: "For families, could something more be done?"

Families "forever" was too long (that would be a fee tail). But could something else for families be allowed? Protecting later generations, after all, was part of the human heart.

We can't give families too long. Anything like "forever" won't do. But can we give them, at least, more than a single generation?

E. Questions for the Common Law

Now come questions for the common law:

- Was there a way to give more time to families?

- In particular, was there a way—without doing away with markets or fee simples—to make this work?

- If so, how long should it be?

The famous answer of the common law comes next. It will create new estate-planning tools for families. Most important, it will create future interests. It will create trusts and wills, too.

In the end, the common law will create, for families, new legal space in what otherwise would be a fee simple world.

And, ultimately, that will lead us to the Rule.

CHAPTER 6

The Legal Setting of the Rule—Future Interests, Conditions, & Contingent Title

We're almost there. The larger "families vs. markets" debate continues. But now comes the specific setting of the Rule.

The common law, as it's prone to do, gets creative. It puts together something new for families inside the fee simple world. And it's something that allows control over multiple generations.

It all involves three things:

- **Future Interests.** Future interests let donors control property over time (and after their own death).

- **Conditions.** Donors then put conditions on future interests as a way to plan for different futures.

- **Contingent Title.** While those conditions are unresolved, future title is contingent.

Then, we get the place of the Rule:

- **The Rule.** The Rule limits how long those conditions (and thus contingent title) can exist.

Now, let's see how this all works.

A. Families & Future Interests—a New Form of Multi-Generational Property

Future interests help families. That's why they were created. In effect, future interests were a legal countermove to the unadorned fee simple.

The legal trick was striking simple: take the fee simple and divide it over time. We still have the fee simple. Now, it's just in pieces, tied together over multiple lifetimes.

One person gets something "now," while another person gets "the rest" later. And the donor gets to decide who those people are.

Now, here's the key: by dividing property over time, future interests created a way for donors to control *multiple* generations. It's a new form of multi-generational property, created for families.

To illustrate, let's first see the options families had if limited to fee simples. Then, let's compare what families could do with future interests—here, a life estate and remainder.

B. The Hypothetical Fate of Families in a Fee-Simple-Only World

In a fee-simple-only world, it's difficult for parents, after their own death, to protect their children. Each generation would be separate. Any legal power the parents had stopped at death. After that, the children would be on their own.

Here's how it would work:

- **Each Generation on Its Own.** Wealth only could be passed, hand-to-hand, one generation at a time. Parents could give property, at death, to their children. But, after that, the children were on their own.

- **Wills Only.** For estate planning, there only would be wills. There was no need for anything more. The only choice: who got property immediately? After that, control was gone.

- **Family Wealth Unprotected.** Once given to the next generation, family wealth was unprotected. Markets could apply any time. The child could sell it any time. Creditors could get it, too.

- **Limited "Family" Ownership.** Continued ownership by later generations could not be guaranteed. The family, as a family, had no legal claim.

Thus, in a fee-simple-only world, families would have a limited role. One generation could not protect another. Plus, the types of donative gifts would be limited.

C. Families & Future Interests—Life Estate & Remainder as Example

In contrast, with future interests, a family could extend control over time. Property also could be kept in the family.

For example, a parent, in a will, could give "a life estate to my child A, remainder to A's children." Note what this lets the donor do:

- Control who gets property years after their own death.

- Keep property in the family for two generations.

Once enough time has passed, of course, the fee simple comes back. But during that period, the donor controls the property and it stays in the family.

For families, this provided a big improvement over the unadorned fee simple. At the same time, it didn't have the deep problems of the fee tail.

Above all, this was something new. Now, donors had a new form of multi-generational property. Unlike the fee tail, too, owners could control it. There was freedom of disposition. And, now, it could reach into the future.

D. An Aside—the Special Role of Trusts

Trusts and future interests go together. They arrive, roughly, at the same time. It's no surprise.

Future interests allow donors to control property after death. But how are they going to do it?

Trusts & Multiple Generations. The answer of the common law, of course, was the trust. Wills let donors speak at death. But trusts do more. Trusts not only let donors speak at death, but for several generations after.

In one legal place, trusts had everything the donor needed:

- A continuing legal entity to "own" property on the donor's behalf for the benefit of beneficiaries (i.e., the trust).

- A way to recognize, memorialize, and keep in place instructions from the donor (i.e., the trust instrument).

- A legal person to watch over it (i.e., the trustee).

Thus, trusts foster legal control of multi-generational property. That's why virtually all future interests today are in trusts.

Now, back to future interests.

E. The Role of Conditions in Future Interests— Planning for Multiple Futures

Future interests also brought with them something else. For donors, it was simple, but important: the prospect of multiple futures.

No one knew, of course, what life would bring after their own death for family left behind. But now, with future interests, it legally mattered.

Before, with fee simples, everything was left to the new owner. And, for fee tails, everything was already fixed; it just was a matter of adding new generations.

But now donors had to plan. Life was always uncertain. No one could control human nature, fate, or the stars. Depending on what happened or not in the future, they needed plans.

To plan for those different futures, though, donors needed options. And to do that, donors needed to think about different sets of alternative futures.

In plain language, donors had thoughts like these:

- I want this to go to A, but if "this" happens to A, then I want it to go to B, instead.

- I want it to go to A, and then to B, but if "this" happens to B after my death, I want it to go to C, instead.

The "this," of course, could be any kind of human happening. It might be good fortune or ill. It might be marriages or births. It might be deaths or divorces. But it could be anything else that worried the donor, too.

F. Conditions & the Central Problem of Contingent Title

Now we get to a critical part.

At some future time, the condition will decide where the property goes. If "this" happens, the property will go one way. But if it doesn't, the property will go to another. That's the whole idea.

Conditions & Contingent Title. Until we know the answer, however, ultimate title is *contingent*. It could go one way or it could go another. We just don't know. If we asked, "So, who owns that future interest?" the answer would be, "I'm not sure yet, we just have to wait." Ultimate title sits in the future, unresolved.

Contingent Title & Markets. But contingent title, in turn, also limits markets. Here's why:

- As long as conditions remain unresolved, title remains contingent.

- As long as title is contingent, property is tied up. Full markets can't apply. And property is in limbo.

G. Families vs. Markets Revisited

Now comes an important question: "how long" should this go on? How long, in this context, should the law let contingent title continue? And why?

Significantly, whatever the answer, it will be yet another example of "families vs. markets." Here's why:

- By using conditions, the donor can keep property in the family and off the market.

- The longer the contingency allowed, the more time families get and the longer markets have to wait.

- The length of the contingency allowed decides the legal balance.

Thus, the choice of "how long" for a contingency is a choice between "how long" for families and "how soon" for markets. What it gives to one, it takes from the other.

Once again, it's families versus markets.

H. A Matter of Perpetuities (or Not)

One final thing. Now, there's an extra twist.

To legal eyes, what families wanted—future interests with conditions—also hinted of something else. And that something else was the fee tail. Why? Because as long as contingencies remained unresolved, property stayed in the family and off the market.

The fee tail itself was "families forever." It was generation after generation, without natural legal end. It took "how long" to its extreme. But the fee tail no longer had the blessing of law. It could not come back. That was agreed.

But now, with future interests and conditions, there's a new question: could something "less than forever" still be "too much" for families? Whatever families got, it couldn't look too much like a fee tail.

Why? Because that would be a "perpetuity."

Ultimately, that's what brings us to the Rule.

CHAPTER 7

The Family That Started It All—the *Duke of Norfolk's Case*

We love to tell the old, old story of its tangled history.

—W. Barton Leach, *Perpetuities in a Nutshell*,
51 Harv. L. Rev. 638, 638 (1938)

A. The Start of the Common-Law Rule

We need a legal answer to "how long" for families. Some concession to families seems reasonable. But if it goes for too long, it ties up property and works like a fee tail.

The answer, when we have it, will tell us:

- How long contingencies in future interests can exist.

- How long donors can keep property in the family.

- How long markets can be delayed.

So, how should we divide between families and markets? And how, too, should all this be done? What standard do we use? How do we measure such a thing? And how will we know if it's right?

The answer of the common law starts with the *Duke of Norfolk's Case*, and that's what we'll look at next.

B. The *Duke of Norfolk's Case*[1]

The creation story for the Rule against Perpetuities we know today is the *Duke of Norfolk's Case*.[2] It takes a case with future interests and conditions, and it give us a "how long" that's still at the heart of the Rule. It also will illustrate the "families vs. markets" debate at the center of the Rule.

When opened, it tells a family story in the thick and threaded words of old common-law conveyancing, all some 350 years past. To the modern reader, it may seem so much dust on the page.

But life really was not so different then. So often—then and now—it's about families. And the daily thoughts of parents, forever, have been to protect their children.

The same story, I am sure, could be told again today. And it's that same story, told again and again, that stands at the heart of the Rule against Perpetuities.

Understand this one story and you will understand so many.

1. The Family

In 1647, Henry Frederick Howard, the 22nd Earl of Arundel, was a wealthy man. Born to an important family, with roots back before the Norman Conquest, he had nine sons and three daughters. A careful and caring parent, he wanted to help his children after his death. The Earl didn't have the stocks and bonds of today. But he did have the one asset best suited for preserving wealth and providing income in 17th century England—land and estates.

---

[1]   The full intrigue and politics of the case are well told in Herbert Barry, *The Duke of Norfolk's Case*, 23 Va. L. Rev. 538 (1937).

[2]   22 Eng. Rep. 931 (Ch. 1682).

2. The Problem

But the Earl also had a special problem. His eldest son, Thomas, then only 20, was mentally ill. As such, the Earl knew, in cold reality, it was unlikely his first-born son would marry and have children. In 17th century England, that mattered: if Thomas's line ended, the earldom of Arundel would go, instead, to the Earl's second son, Henry.

3. The Contingency

But as the Earl also knew, the fate of the earldom of Arundel likely would not play out for decades. After all, Thomas, the eldest son, was only in his early 20s. And it wasn't certain the second son, Henry, would outlive his older brother Thomas, either; Henry was only 16 months younger.

To ease his mind, the Earl made a contingency plan. It had two parts:

- First, in the interim, the Earl wanted to support Henry. For this, he wanted to give Henry the barony of Grostock. With this, the Earl could give Henry a source of income while the future of Arundel was being decided.

- Second, the Earl also wanted something else later. And, ultimately, this was the key provision. If, as expected, Henry later inherited the earldom of Arundel, then the Earl wanted the barony of Grostock to shift, instead, to his third son, Charles. This way, the Earl could even out benefits for his children.

All in all, the plan resembled the child's game of musical chairs: Henry got Grostock, but if Henry also got Arundel later, then Charles got Grostock, instead.

Equally important, the Earl knew he'd probably die before he knew the answer.

4. The Legal Document & Lawyers

For help, the Earl went to one of the best conveyancers in England, Sir Orlando Bridgeman. In response, Bridgeman drew up a trust and conveyance in essentially the following form:

> The barony of Grostock to Henry and his heirs, but if Thomas dies without issue during the life of Henry, then to Charles and his heirs.

In the argot of future interests, Bridgeman conveyed Grostock to Henry subject to a *shifting executory limitation* in favor of Charles.

5. How Events Played Out

Afterwards, events played out as the Earl anticipated:

- In 1652, five years after the conveyance, the Earl died. He never knew the fate of his sons.

- In 1677, twenty-five years after the Earl's death, the contingencies finally got resolved. Thomas died without children while Henry was still alive.[3] Thus, on the death of Thomas, the earldom of Arundel went to Henry.

Under the terms of the trust—and now some 25 years later—the barony of Grostock should shift from Henry to Charles.

But here things turn sour. Despite the terms of the conveyance, Henry decided to keep the barony of Grostock.

---

[3]   Henry was not without action here. After the death of their father, Henry kept Thomas locked away in a private asylum in Padua, Italy. Herbert Barry, *supra* note 1, at 543 n.8. That's one way to prevent your older brother from producing an heir.

We don't know why. Perhaps he was greedy. Perhaps it was part of the family feud he ignited, just the year before, when he married his low-born mistress. But, perhaps, too, Henry was just flexing raw power. Thanks to recent politics, he was now the 6th Duke of Norfolk, holder of the most powerful peerage in England.

Understandably, Charles, the younger brother, was upset. His father had promised him the barony of Grostock, and Charles had waited, patiently, for 25 years. Even more stinging, Charles knew his older brother Henry didn't need it. Between brothers, it must have seemed stingy, cold, and cruel.

Thus, when Henry kept the barony of Grostock, Charles went to court.

C. The Equities & the Chancellor

Based on the law of the day, Henry's argument for keeping Grostock was this: the condition giving it to Charles was invalid as a "perpetuity." He could cite somewhat similar cases, too.

But the basic equities of the case were troublesome. The Earl's goal was laudable and human: to protect his children. The events were likely, even probable. The Earl also used an experienced conveyancer. On the other side, too, was a selfish son.

These equities came before no ordinary judge—Lord Chancellor Nottingham. A respected scholar, he'd written two books on Equity and helped draft the Statute of Frauds.

Nottingham had survived big cases with big personalities before, too. Just the year before, he'd presided in the House of Lords when Henry's uncle, as part of the Popish Plot, was charged with high treason against the King.[4]

---

[4]   With Nottingham presiding at trial, the House of Lords voted to convict. The original sentence: drawing and quartering, the most gruesome penalty of the day. In an act of mercy, the King (Charles II) reduced it to beheading.

Against all this, the Chancellor might have thought the case before him a simple one. The case raised a pressing domestic issue of the day: splitting property between parents and children. And, here, too, the Chancellor had five children. He was going to speak his mind.

1. The Equities of the Case

Getting straight to the equities, Nottingham started by scolding Henry. He had some stinging words:

> It is a very hard thing for a son to tell his father that the provision he has made for your younger brothers is void in law.[5]

And then he told Henry, frankly and openly, how hard it would be in his court:

> [B]ut it is much harder for him to tell him so in Chancery. And if such a provision be void, it had need to be void with a vengeance.[6]

Moving to the merits, Nottingham framed the question as one about parents taking care of children. Why shouldn't the Earl be allowed, he asked, "to provide for the contingencies of his own family that are in immediate prospect"?[7]

2. The Answer in the Case

But how was "immediate prospect" to be measured? Here, Nottingham used a famous—and unusual—measure still with us today. The contingencies, he said, would be resolved "within the compass of a life."[8]

---

[5] *Duke of Norfolk's Case*, 22 Eng. Rep. at 953.
[6] Id.
[7] Id. at 955.
[8] Id. at 951.

[A Modern Aside. And note here how they would. When the Earl made the conveyance, he didn't know how the contingency—"if Thomas die without issue while Henry lives"—would come out. That was the whole point. Thomas might or might not have children and Thomas might or might not die before Henry. But both contingencies would be resolved—one way or the other—during the life of Thomas.]

Thus, Nottingham famously concluded, "where it is within the compass of one life, that the contingency is to happen, there is no danger of a perpetuity."[9]

That was enough to decide the case. Since all contingencies here would be resolved "within the compass" of Thomas's life, it was not a perpetuity. Charles got the barony of Grostock.

3. Musings on Longer Periods

But what after this?

Right here, you could see the next Socratic question coming. If Nottingham allowed contingencies for "the compass of a life," then where would it stop? What was the natural end?

Perhaps parroting questions from Henry's lawyer, the record continues:

But what time? And where are the bounds of that contingency? You may limit, it seems, upon a contingency to happen in a life. What if it be limited, if such a one die without issue within twenty-one years, or 100 years, or while *Westminster-Hall* stands? Where will you stop, if you do not stop here?[10]

---

[9]   Id. at 950.
[10]   Id. at 960.

Nottingham did not welcome the question. He felt so strongly about the merits of this case, he wasn't going to worry about the next case. Thus, in his response, Nottingham famously slips the issue. Still, you can almost hear the emotion in his voice:

> I will tell you where I will stop: I will stop wherever any visible inconvenience doth appear; for the just bounds of a fee simple upon a fee simple are not yet determined, but the first inconvenience that ariseth upon it will regulate it.[11]

All Nottingham seems to say is, "I'll know it when I see it." Beyond that most general guide, however, he was done.

D. The Secret to Understanding the Case— a Rule *for* Perpetuities & Families

While always cited for establishing a rule *against* perpetuities, the *Duke of Norfolk's Case* didn't strike down anything. Instead, it extended the right to control land within a family beyond what existing law arguably allowed.

What Nottingham said, which so often is missed, is this: if we need to wait, after your death, to see what happens to your children, that's fine. That's not too long. We'll give that to families.

Nottingham allowed families, in the interest of estate planning, to control property given to the next generation. The Earl of Arundel didn't know what the fate of his sons would be. No one did. But now, at least, the Earl could plan. And for that "compass of a life" after, he could keep markets at bay. Until it was resolved, too, Arundel would stay in the family.

For parents doing this, Nottingham concluded, the law should allow some legal space. It was parents, after their own death,

---

[11] Id.

watching over the full lifetimes of their children. For families, he decided, that was not "too much."

Thus, Nottingham sanctioned "a rule for perpetuities rather than a rule against perpetuities."[12] In effect, he gave families a *limited* fee tail or a *limited* perpetuity.

1. Families & Contingent Title—Why It Matters

Ultimately, of course, the Rule was about contingent title. Let's return to the contingency in the case:

> Grostock to Henry, but if Thomas dies without issue during the life of Henry, then to Charles.

During Thomas's life, title to Grostock is contingent. Henry owns Grostock, but title may shift later to Charles. It all depends on what happens to another person, Thomas.

But here's the critical point: families as families, may seek inalienability. Here, contingent title reinforces the family unit. Outside buyers are deterred. Until the contingency is resolved, Grostock is unmarketable. And, thus, title is inalienable.

Most important, contingent title keeps any wealth generated, locked, within the family. For how long? For as long as the contingency remains unresolved.

2. Nottingham, Families, & Inalienability

That's why the Rule mattered so much in the *Duke of Norfolk's Case*. The property would stay in the family and be inalienable for the term of the contingency. This was why lawyers hinted a perpetuity was possible.

---

[12] Restatement (Second) of Property: Donative Transfers, Part I, The Rule Against Perpetuities and Related Rules as Applied to Donative Transfers 10 (1983).

The worry was about the return, in new form, of the perpetuity of old, the fee tail. If property could be kept in the family, inalienable, for the term of a contingency, what might that contingency be? If, as Nottingham was asked, it might be whether a person "die without issue . . . while *Westminster-Hall* stands,"[13] then fee tails would be back.

Nottingham famously limited contingencies to the "compass of a life." But he did so as a concession to families.

Thus, the *Duke of Norfolk's Case* created—for families—a place between the full *alienability* of a fee simple at each generation and the full *inalienability* of a fee tail. And it was all because of contingencies.

3. The Heart of the Rule

In the end, this one point—a limited period of inalienability as a concession to family unity and strategic planning—is the heart of the Rule. The basic period is taken as given. Only when inalienability *exceeds* the base period do perpetuities appear.

It's a simple idea. And the Rule spins on this point. Always keep it in mind.

E. Principles of the *Duke of Norfolk's Case*

Chancellor Nottingham never talked about perpetuities again. Little more than a year later, he was dead.

But his voice, speaking through the facts of the case, set principles still with us today:

- **Donative Transfers & Families.** Fundamentally, the Rule's about donative transfers within the family. It's about people trying, in a slice of time, to map

---

[13] Id. at 960.

possible futures. After my death, how can I care for my children? Will there be marriages or babies? When will death come? Who may be blessed or not?

- **Contingencies as Multiple Futures.** Contingencies are nothing more than multiple futures. At the time they're made, we don't have answers. That's why we make them.

- **Will It Be Resolved?** What matters for contingencies is this: one way or the other, we will know. No one answer is preordained, but some answer is.

- **The Measure for Resolution.** Nottingham said answers must come within the "compass of a life." Often, this part of the Rule still mystifies. But it shouldn't. The measure comes from planning for families and generations.

F. The Original Rule—Life in Being—One Generation

The Rule against Perpetuities is one about *generations*. The original rule in the *Duke of Norfolk's Case* was this: if you knew the person, contingencies about them could be resolved after your death. In essence, this meant one generation, with generation defined as people alive when the conveyance was made.

It was an elegant and simple rule. It also would have been easy to apply.

But the case also left open what, if anything, might come after Nottingham's rule. How long could a family tie up land? When, exactly, did a "visible inconvenience" appear? Was the *Duke of Norfolk's Case* itself the edge? Or was the edge still later?

G. The Extended Rule—Life in Being plus 21 Years

It took 150 years to get the answer. By 1833, the final piece fell into place—an additional 21 years.

Why 21 years? First cases involved children in gestation, along with time to reach majority, hence the 21. Later, the circle widened to a general, free-floating period of 21 years. This was deemed a "reasonable time" after lives in being, even if not linked to a particular beneficiary.[14]

Thus, the period of "a life in being plus 21 years" became how long families could keep property inalienable. After that, it must be ended.

H. The Extended Rule & Unborn Grandchildren

The extra 21-year period also meant this: now yet-to-be-born grandchildren could be included as well. Under the extended Rule, a person could help "all of those in his family he personally knew and the first generation after them upon attaining majority."[15]

But there also was a rub. For any after-born grandchildren, any contingency needed resolution within 21 years. They didn't get a full lifetime, like the children or grandchildren born before. In short, not all grandchildren were treated the same. This would bring problems later.[16]

---

[14]   Cadell v Palmer, 6 Eng. Rep. 956 (H.L. 1833).

[15]   W. Barton Leach, 6 American Law of Property § 24.16, at 51 (A. James Casner ed. 1952).

[16]   See Chapter 12, at 118 (classic traps); Chapter 17, at 179 (two full generations of *Restatement (3d) of Property*).

I.   The Final Core of the Rule—Two Generations

Fundamentally, the Rule's about *two generations*. That's been the measure for the last 150 years.

As we'll later see, people may argue about when a generation starts or ends. Is it tied to real people or fixed periods of time? Then, too, are events in it hypothetical or real?

But it's a fundamental part of the Rule. It remains, even today, at its core.

CHAPTER 8

How the *Duke of Norfolk's Case* Became a Special Rule

The *Duke of Norfolk's Case* started the Rule. It used the "the compass of a life" and hinted at limits when "any visible inconvenience" appeared. But where would it go from here?

This chapter traces, briefly, the growth of the Rule from the *Duke of Norfolk's Case* to the final Rule of John Chipman Gray.

Think of it as a map of possibilities. What else could this Rule have become? And how, too, did this Rule become a special rule, different from every other rule in the law? What made it so?

Most important, to use this Rule, why must lawyers change how they think? Why here can't lawyers use their usual "thinking like a lawyer" skills? And why here must lawyers learn, all anew, how to argue?

These are simple and important points. But they're rarely talked about. They're key, though, to understanding the Rule.

A. The Legal Road Not Taken—"Visible Inconvenience" as a Standard (vs. a Rule)

After the *Duke of Norfolk's Case*, no one path was obvious. While perpetuities law today is about a famous "rule," it didn't have to be that way. In truth, it could have taken very different legal form.

Instead of a rule, perpetuities law might have become a classic common-law standard. There could have been decisions, case-by-case, whether a "visible inconvenience" had occurred. It could, too, have been a matter of balancing different factors to decide each case.

In application, it would have been like deciding standards for a "reasonable person" in Torts. It all could have turned on various societal standards or policies about markets or families.

But the key was this: had it become a standard, answers about "visible inconvenience" would be case-by-case. And there would be no single correct answer.

In our legal world, of course, that did not happen. The Rule went another way.

But there's a big lesson here: the common-law Rule of John Chipman Gray was not inevitable. It was a choice. From the start, different legal forms were possible. No one form was obvious, either. That matters, too, for thinking about reform.

B. Perpetuities as a Strict Rule Unlike Others of the Common Law

After the *Duke of Norfolk's Case*, courts turned toward rules. Rather than leave "visible inconvenience" open, they eventually defined it as a firm rule: an extra 21 years (and to the day).

The same happened to violations. And here, as well, courts used rules. If, looking forward, a contingency might not happen, it was invalid.

Both were strict rules. This was significant.

Why? Because so many rules you learn in law school are soft rules. They start as general rules or expectations. But then are followed by exceptions, counter-rules, or defenses. Always, there is back-and-forth.

It's everywhere in the common law. It's basic claims (e.g., torts, breach of contract, or trespass) countered with "good reasons" for avoiding them (e.g., consent, impossibility, or necessity).

Thus, when students first come to a "rule," they next expect to see ways around it. Elsewhere in the common law, there are causes of action. And always, too, there are defenses. It's how law typically works.

But not here. And that's important. Here, that oh-so-normal legal thinking doesn't work. Because this rule—this Rule against Perpetuities—is not like the others. Here, there is no back-and-forth.

Instead, if there's a violation here, it's the end. There is no extra step. There are no excuses, defenses, or counter-arguments. It's done.

C. Perpetuities as a Binary World

With that, perpetuities became a binary world. It now was black and white. There was no legal gray. There were no matters of degree, either.

Once given a hard rule without exceptions, there now were only two choices. Either it was inside the circle of lives in being or it wasn't. Here, there is no back-and-forth.

Now, it just was "yes" or "no." It was good or bad. It was one or the other. There was nothing else to say.

Thus, from the start, perpetuities had rules unlike other parts of the common law.

D. Ways of Thinking—Looking Forward Using Hypotheticals

With this, too, came a different kind of thinking. One of the distinctive features of the Rule is this: it operates, looking forward, based on hypotheticals.

Elsewhere in the law, this isn't what "thinking like a lawyer" is like. It isn't what law students do in other classes, either. In truth, it's unlike anything else in the common law.

It's important to see why.

The Rule's not about the past. Instead, it's always forward-looking. The one question: when the contingency starts, looking forward, is it inside the circle of the Rule or not?

The question is not, "What are the facts?" or "What happened here?" Even though, of course, that's the first question law students are trained to ask (and from the first day). But not here.

Instead, it's about, "What's the contingency and who's alive?" From this point forward—and fixed, always, at this point—the question is, "Which side of the legal line is this on?"

E. Ways of Thinking—Not if Some Event Will Happen, but Whether Certain Questions Will Be Answered

Every day, lawyers want to know, looking forward, whether something might "happen." It could be accidents or missed payments. It could be death or divorce, floods or forfeitures. It's what good lawyers do.

But not so with the Rule. For the Rule, the issue isn't whether any particular event will happen. It isn't whether something is probable or likely. It isn't about what we predict the future to be, either. Instead, it's about whether, looking forward, we'll have answers to certain questions.

For perpetuities, those questions are two:

- Will the contingency be resolved within the perpetuities period?

- Is there any possibility it won't?

Ultimately, for each, the answer is either "yes" or "no." And if it's "yes" for one, it's "no" for the other.

F. Ways of Thinking—Not Arguments but Proofs

Right here, the Rule takes a critical turn. And it goes to the heart of the Rule. The question now is this: How do lawyers argue? What can I say to make my case?

But the surprising answer is this: you may think you know how to argue, but you don't. Why? Because arguments about perpetuities are different from other legal arguments.

For law students, this seems strange. From the first day, you're taught "how to make arguments." It's the most enduring skill you learn.

By now, you can argue about facts and cases. You can parse words and rules. And you know how to make policy arguments, too. You do it every day.

But here's the key: when it comes to the Rule, you don't do any of those things. Instead, it's something you never did before in law school. Until trained, no lawyer naturally knows how to do it, either.

For perpetuities, there's always a single, right answer. It isn't debatable, either. Both sides, on the facts, should always get the same answer. It's just a matter of doing proofs, one or the other, to see what it is. Once found, it's over.

The arguments you make are special, too. They are not what lawyers normally do. They are *logical proofs*. They take the form of math puzzles or geometry proofs.

These logical proofs also come with special assumptions used nowhere else in the law. Some are about whether people, even the very old, may yet have children. Others are about whether different people might die together, all in an instant. Some are fanciful, others may be false. But they're all used.

Whatever else you've learned in law school, you haven't learned this. It's all new. But knowing that it's new is the start.

G. Then Along Came John Chipman Gray

We'll look next at the full common-law Rule and how it operated in practice. Much will be about one book written by one person—John Chipman Gray.

But, even now, you know much of what the outline will be.

PART 4

The Common-Law Rule
of John Chipman Gray

CHAPTER 9

An Interlude—
Personalities—John
Chipman Gray

A. Why John Chipman Gray & His Rule Still Matter

Lord Nottingham started the telling of a common-law Rule against Perpetuities in the *Duke of Norfolk's Case*. But John Chipman Gray finished it, 200 years later, in his famous treatise *The Rule Against Perpetuities*.[1] Once done, Gray's version of the Rule would be ruthless, dogmatic, and formalistic.

Gray's influence was immense. He dominated the field. He wrote the most famous book ever on the common-law Rule against Perpetuities. In truth, he crystallized it.

The rule—as he drafted it—*became* the common-law rule. Courts cited him instead of cases. For lawyers and judges, the Rule

---

[1] John Chipman Gray, The Rule Against Perpetuities (4th ed. 1942).

against Perpetuities was whatever John Chipman Gray said it was. He was "the high priest of the Rule Against Perpetuities."[2]

Even today, Gray's rule is used as a baseline in the Uniform Statutory Rule against Perpetuities, enacted in over half the states today. Plus, under any of the many modern reforms, if you comply with Gray's Rule, the interest is valid.

It matters, even now.

B. John Chipman Gray & His Book

Gray was a force of personality. He fought in the Civil War and rose to the rank of Major. In 1865, he started his own law firm, Ropes & Gray, which, so-titled, still exists today.[3]

He started teaching at Harvard in 1869 as a Lecturer, since he was still practicing law. Seven years later, in 1875, he had an endowed chair. By the time he retired from teaching in 1913, all the members of the law school faculty had been his students.

A contemporary of Langdell, Gray wrote the very first casebook on Property. It was six volumes long and totaled over 4000 pages. Gray's students took six semesters of Property. That broke down to one volume of his casebook a semester. Today, it would be a 12-credit class. Gray's casebook had over 60 cases on the Rule against Perpetuities, covering almost 300 pages.[4]

His famous book, *The Rule Against Perpetuities*, was the work of a lifetime. Over 30 years, Gray wrote three editions. The first was published in 1886, two years before his casebook. The second

---

[2] George L. Haskins, *Extending the Grasp of the Dead Hand: Reflections on the Origins of the Rule Against Perpetuities*, 125 U. Pa. L. Rev. 19, 21 n.7 (1977).

[3] What Gray might have thought about his law firm lasting longer than all lives then in being plus 21 years, we don't know.

[4] See John Chipman Gray, 5 Select Cases and other Authorities on the Law of Property 425-717 (2d ed. 1909). And his students didn't have the book you're reading now.

came twenty years later, in 1906, and the third in 1915, two years before his death. Each was carefully revised and expanded. In those three decades, Gray added over 200 pages to the text.

The 4th edition, the one most cited today, was updated 25 years after his death by his son, Roland Gray. The 4th edition remains in print today, offered as a legal classic.[5]

C. What Gray Did About Perpetuities

Before Gray, "perpetuities" was a sprawling and varied pocket of law. The *Duke of Norfolk's Case* surely was part of it. But so were many other vague and varied rules about tying up property. There was talk about such things as "a possibility on a possibility" or new entails, and others.

Gray changed that. Among other things, here's what he did:

- **Trimming and Codifying the Rule.** Gray distilled the rule into cleaner and fewer parts. Rather than "a" rule, among others, about alienability of property, it became "the" Rule against Perpetuities.

- **A Single Sentence.** Consistent with the growing academic style of the time, Gray sought out the "true" principle of the Rule. He then put it in a single sentence.

- **Separate Rules.** Gray distinguished the Rule against Perpetuities from the Rule against Suspension of the Power of Alienation.[6] Previously, many had conflated the two. He even wrote a separate book about it.[7]

---

[5]   As a work now in the public domain, numerous hard-copy reprints and reissues exist. Somewhere in the world, I am sure, it sits on someone's Kindle.

[6]   Chapter 14, at page 153.

[7]   John Chipman Gray, Restraints on the Alienation of Property (2d ed. 1895).

He did all this, too, at a critical time for the Rule. Not long before Gray wrote his book, big doctrinal parts of the Rule finally had fallen into place. There was an emerging literature on perpetuities, too.

It was ripe for work.

D. John Chipman Gray as a Product of His Times

But Gray also was a product of his times. He wrote in the decades after the Civil War. And, here, the influences tell. The Rule he drafted carried with it the intellectual marks of the age.

Living in the most formalist era in American law,[8] Gray would craft, write, and defend—without guilt—the most formalistic rule ever in the common law.

As so often in law, big ideas matter. To understand Gray's rule and its place, two will matter most:

- His rule would not be a rule of policy or even a rule of law: it would be a rule of *math*.

- His rule would be one of *Property* rather than donative transfers.

Both would have consequences.

But first Gray's common-law rule, in all its formalistic glory.

---

[8] See Donald Gjerdingen, *The Future of Our Past: The Legal Mind and the Legacy of Classical Common-Law Thought*, 68 Ind. L.J. 743, 750-63 (1993).

CHAPTER 10

Gray's Common-Law Rule—the Nutshell

A. The Place of the Common-Law Rule

After studying the classic common-law Rule, we will look at modern reforms. But even modern reforms don't leave the common-law Rule behind.

Here's why:

- **Compliance with Common-Law Rule as Preferred.** Modern reforms don't change the Rule. Instead, they change what happens when lawyers violate it. The lesson here: if you comply with the common-law Rule, you don't need any reforms or backup.

- **Modern Reforms.** No modern reform can be understood without first understanding the common-law Rule. In short, you can't just start with modern reforms. Instead, you must start with the classic Rule and move forward.

- **Continued Relevance.** The law must always balance control of property between generations. The issue will never go away. Abolishing the Rule won't change that. Instead, questions will just shift to a different place. Thus, any reform or alternatives must start with the common-law Rule, too.

This chapter and the next two cover just the basics of the classic common-law Rule. Later, in Chapter 14, we'll consider advanced issues such as applying the Rule to class gifts, charities, and powers of appointment.

B. The Classic Text of the Rule

John Chipman Gray penned the classic statement of the Rule over a hundred years ago:

> No interest is good unless it must vest, if at all, not later than twenty-one years after some life in being at the creation of the interest.[1]

Know these words by heart. Every good law student does.

C. What's the Rule About?

The Rule itself is about a critical issue of justice between generations: how many generations into the future can one generation control property? For Gray, the Rule was "*the* law of future interests."[2]

The Rule is often classified as a rule against the *remoteness of vesting*. The Rule requires uncertainties about the state of title to be resolved within a given time, typically two generations. If not, then the interest is void, and thus determined another way.

---

[1] John Chipman Gray, The Rule Against Perpetuities § 201, at 191 (4th ed. 1942).

[2] Id. at ix (emphasis in original).

In a typical perpetuities setting, a person puts contingencies in property if certain events come to pass. Often this is a will or a trust, with gifts or interests promised on certain events, such as the birth of a child or a beneficiary living to a certain age. But if the person pushes the contingency too far into the future—and thus leaves the interest unresolved for too long—the interest is void.

The Rule also indirectly limits the duration of trusts. In effect, the Rule requires all beneficiaries be identified within a certain period. Once past the perpetuities period, the beneficiaries can terminate the trust, even against the wishes of the settlor.

D. Interests Subject to the Rule

Before you worry about the Rule against Perpetuities, you first must know whether it potentially applies. Fundamentally, the Rule considers contingencies in certain property interests. This requires:

- A property interest (i.e., not a contract).

- An interest created in the transferee (i.e., either a remainder or an executory interest). This excludes a reversion, possibility of reverter, or right of entry, since each creates interests in the transferor.

- An interest subject to a contingency (i.e., not vested).

I assume you know estates in land from your first-year Property course and your experience there with variously-bundled sticks and future interests.

But here are a few tips:

- **Future Interests vs. the Rule.** Future interests are one thing, the Rule is another. If you have problems, think first about future interests. That's where most learning gets stuck. One is a legal maze (i.e., future interests) and the other isn't (i.e., the Rule).

- **Future Interests Not Subject to the Rule.** Not all future interests are subject to the Rule. That helps. If something could go back to the grantor (i.e., possibility of reverter or right of entry), the Rule doesn't apply.[3]

- **Interests Subject to the Rule—Gifts to 3d Persons.** The interests subject to the Rule all go to third persons. These are the kind of gifts, of course, that normally happen in wills and trusts.

- **Contingent Remainders & Executory Interests.** The Rule most often applies to contingent remainders and executory interests. Both interests go to third persons. Both, too, use conditions. Significantly, the *Restatement (3d) of Property* collapses the distinction between the two.[4] Both are contingent interests to third persons.

- **Conditions (or Not).** The Rule only applies to conditions. Why? Without conditions, there's no contingent title. The basic question is this: "Is there more than one path for future title?" If so, it's contingent. And the Rule matters.

- **"Vested."** In contrast, if there's only one path—if we already know who gets it and when—then it's

---

[3]   A side note: conditions here may complicate title, too. But they typically have their own statutes limiting the length of the condition. It's a similar idea, just not the Rule.

[4]   Restatement (Third) of Property: Wills and Other Donative Transfers § 25.2 comment c (2011). To no surprise, it all had been predicted some 60 years ago by Jessie Dukeminier. See Jessie Dukeminier, *Contingent Remainders and Executory Interests: A Requiem for the Distinction*, 44 Minn. L. Rev. 13 (1958).

"vested." Here, the Rule isn't needed because there's not contingent title.

- **"Subject to Open."** The Rule also applies to "vested interests subject to open." Once again, while this sounds complex, it's not. It's just about "yet-to-be-born" beneficiaries and the special *all-or-nothing rule* for class gifts.[5]

Once all these elements are put in play, you must ask whether any contingent interest violates the Rule.

E. Basic Questions About the Rule

1. What Must Happen During the Period?

The Rule requires certain contingencies be resolved within a certain time. If the contingency can't be resolved, it's void.

The key term is *resolved*. The text of the Rule says interests must vest "if at all" during the period. The "if at all" language is critical. The contingency need not happen, but it must be resolved, i.e., we must know whether or not it will happen. Once the contingency is resolved, interests and beneficiaries are determined.

Here, the Rule is subject to a special and famous constraint: the validity of the interest is judged only at the moment of its creation, not later. Under the classic Rule, the only relevant legal time is the *effective date* of the instrument. Nothing else matters. Not what happened before, and not what happened after.

From this point, only what *could* happen looking forward from the start of the period matters. What really happens after the

---

[5]   See Chapter 14, page 148 (class gifts). If not for the all-or-nothing rule (and there were other options), "vested subject to open" wouldn't apply.

effective date is ignored. Of course, that goes against legal common sense. But it's also a key feature of the Rule.

When considering whether the contingency will be resolved, all that matters is *logical proof*. Probabilities, hunches, or beliefs do not count. Hard, exact, precise answers exist here, and only hard, exact, precise answers.

Looking at the contingency, there are only two choices:

- **Valid.** The contingency absolutely will be resolved during the perpetuities period.

  Or

- **Invalid.** There is some possibility, however remote, the contingency will not be resolved during the perpetuities period. Here, any amount of uncertainty is fatal.

One or the other choice applies in every case. If the contingency will be resolved during the period, the interest is valid. But if there's some possibility, however remote, the contingency won't be resolved, the interest is invalid. It's that simple.

This method of logical proof gives the Rule its math-like quality. It also goes against legal common sense. From your first law classes onward, you were told—again and again—the law does not have clear rules. This is an exception. Enjoy it.

2. When Does the Period Start?

The legal clock for the Rule starts ticking on the *effective date* of the instrument. This sets the start of the perpetuities period. Once this date is set, the Rule is applied on the effective date, looking forward. As stated by Gray in his Rule, the critical time is "at the creation of the interest."

Under the Rule, the effective date depends on the type of instrument. For example:

- **Wills & Revocable Trusts.** For a will, the effective date is when the testator dies. Until then, the will could be revoked. The same rule applies to a testamentary trust or a revocable inter vivos trust.

- **Irrevocable Trusts & Deeds.** In contrast, the effective date for an irrevocable inter vivos trust is when the instrument is executed. The same rule applies to a deed. Both are effective when executed. Note, too, the person making the contingency here (e.g., the settlor or grantor) is still alive on the effective date, unlike a will or revocable trust.

This also means the effective date for the Rule could differ based on the choice of instrument. Understanding the effective date is one of the keys to understanding the Rule.

This simple point plays into some famous traps set by the Rule. For example, while a will becomes effective when the testator dies, an identical interest in an irrevocable inter vivos trust becomes effective a generation earlier—when the settlor is still alive. By using an irrevocable trust rather than a will, therefore, the effective date shifts forward a generation. This is no small point, and must be carefully watched.

Of course, legal common sense typically considers only when a document is signed or when it says it becomes effective. As much sense as this makes elsewhere in the law, this can be a fatal mistake when hunting perpetuities.

3. How Long Is the Period?

This is one of the unusual parts of the Rule. While legal rules typically measure time by dates certain (e.g., August 8) or set periods of time (e.g., 30 days or 10 years), the Rule against Perpetuities does not. Instead, it marks time by generations.

The legal clock set by the common-law Rule against Perpetuities is the darkly poetic phrase *lives in being plus 21 years.* This basically means two generations. The first generation is someone alive on the effective date of the instrument. This is known as a *life in being* or a *validating life.* The second generation is the extra 21 years. It's a partial generation.

Of course, this way of stating the Rule grates against legal common sense. Lawyers think first of set periods—whether it be 30 days, one year, or 20 years—to apply to classes of events. They are used to filing deadlines, statutes of limitation, or terms in contracts. But that does not matter here.

4. Periods of Gestation

A fine point must be covered. The perpetuities period includes periods of gestation where appropriate. Thus, a life in being could include a person in gestation on the effective date. Similarly, when the 21-year period ends, a child in gestation may take as a beneficiary. In an appropriate case, therefore, the period could be as long as 21 years and 9 months. An example would be a child conceived just before the father died.

F. Basic Questions About Measuring Lives

1. Who Can Be a Measuring Life?

A *life in being* must be a person alive (or in gestation) on the effective date of the instrument. While life in being is the classic term used by John Chipman Gray, other sources use the term *measuring life.* Many modern scholars use the term *validating life* instead to reflect the role it plays in validating interests under the logic of the Rule. When learning the Rule for the first time, thinking about a validating life probably makes the most sense, but understand that the three terms—life in being, measuring life, and validating life—all mean the same thing.

Reflecting the emphasis on generations, a measuring life must be a real person, not a corporation or an animal. The long life of a tortoise or a Sequoia tree cannot be used for a life in being. Neither can the perpetual legal life of a corporation.

Be aware, too, a measuring life may actually be measuring *lives*. If the contingency involves a group of people—for example, the testator's children—the group stands together, collectively, as the measuring lives. As a wonderful old case tells us, "if all the candles be light at once it is good."[6] Thus, here, *life in being* ends with the death of the last survivor of the group.

2. How Do I Know a Measuring Life When I See It?

This is a classic stumbling point for students. Legal common sense tells you important people must be named in the document. Law students expect important people to be named in contracts, complaints, and conveyances. But this principle of legal common sense does not apply to the Rule.

Under the logic of the Rule, the measuring life—and hence the person you need to find—need not be named in the instrument. Of course, the *contingency* will be stated in the instrument, but the measuring life may not be. The language creating a gift or conveyance may mention a person who turns out to be a measuring life. But don't expect the instrument to identify that person as a measuring life.

---

[6]   Love v. Wyndham, 86 Eng. Rep. 724, 726 (K.B. 1670).

3. Name-Your-Own Contingency

Of course, persons could be named as measuring lives in the instrument. This might be done, for example, to maximize the duration of a trust.

For example, a drafter might designate a trust to end 21 years after the death of a certain designated people, say after the deaths of A, B, C, D, E, and F. If it lists a reasonable number of people who are easy to identify, this is valid.

Some famous examples include a dozen healthy newborns or members of a royal family. Naming measuring lives typically would assure an interest lasting about 100 years or more. The same technique, as we will see, is used for saving clauses.

4. If a Measuring Life Is Not Stated, Where Do I Find One?

However reasonable it would be in other legal contexts, don't expect to pick up a will or trust and see a measuring life designated in the instrument. Look instead at the *contingency* in the instrument. Start there. First ask, "If the interest is to vest, *what* must happen"? Then ask yourself, "*Who* could affect this"? If a validating life is to be found, it will be found here. It will be among people alive on the effective date who can affect the contingency.

This is a key to understanding the Rule. Use the contingency to limit where you look for measuring lives. Measuring lives, if found, always link to the contingency.

5. What Types of Contingencies Usually Are Involved?

Often the contingency involves people having children, living to certain ages, or meeting other conditions. Multiple contingencies can exist, too. If so, all must be valid.

After you set the effective date, look at the contingency. When you do, break it down into two parts:

- *What* must be done?

- *Who* must do it? Some contingencies, like the *Duke of Norfolk's Case,* were limited to named persons. Other times, in contrast, the contingency may use an open term like *children* or *grandchildren.*

Often this is a critical part of the analysis. Even after you know the *what,* a small change in the *who* may invalidate an interest. Thus, validity could turn more on *who* must do something than *what* must be done. Pay particular attention to the *who* part of any contingency.

G. If I Violate the Rule, What Are the Consequences?

Under the Rule, if the contingency might not vest, it's void. In contrast, if a validating life can be given, the interest is valid.

The Rule strikes the offending interest from the instrument. In effect, the Rule runs an invalidating line though the language creating the remote interest. The language remaining then is given effect.

Because of this, Gray's Rule often played a disruptive role in estate planning. Since mistakes by lawyers couldn't be corrected, it became a malpractice trap for lawyers.

It also fostered litigation. If dissatisfied relatives could find violations of the Rule in a will or trust, they could use it to attack gifts to other beneficiaries.

After modern reforms, however, much of this has been corrected.

CHAPTER 11

The Cold Heart of Gray's Rule—Two Options & Some Rules of Thumb

In questions of remoteness . . . there is . . . a definite recognized rule: if a decision agrees with it, it is right; if it does not agree with it, it is wrong. In no part of the law is the reasoning so mathematical in its character; none has so small a human element.

—John Chipman Gray, The Rule Against
Perpetuities xi (4th ed. 1942)

A. The Two Answers—Mutually Exclusive

Now we reach the cold heart of the common-law Rule. The Rule has a special logic. It seems strangely parched of human touch. Once laid out, it is not what most law students expect. The heart of the Rule works like a geometry proof.

Again, the heart of the logic—and thus the Rule—is this: in every Rule against Perpetuities case, one of two things must happen:

- **Valid.** Either a validating life can be named.

Or

- **Invalid.** An invalidating story can be told.

These are mutually exclusive.

At times, the first option is labeled the *validating* side of the Rule, while the second option is labeled the *invalidating* side of the Rule.

One or the other happens in every case. Either you can point to a validating life or you can tell an invalidating story using the ritualized storyline. If you can do one, you can't do the other. It's that simple.

B. The Two Choices—Picking Sides

Again, these two choices are mutually exclusive. In every case, you have one or the other. Sounds easy enough and it is.

But the problem is this: you don't know at first *which* one you have. And because of the special logic of the Rule, there is a special consequence: if you jump the wrong way, you'll never find your answer.

Thus, the key is which side to try first. You have to jump to one side of the fence or the other. If you jump the right way, you're done. But if you jump the wrong way and don't know it, you'll never get an answer. You'll wander, forever, in a legal thicket.

C. Making a Good First Guess Which Way to Jump

In planning which way to jump, think about these three rules of thumb:

- **Nottingham's Rule.** Is the contingency limited to a named, living person? If so, it's valid. The contingency is guaranteed to be resolved during the compass of that person's life.

- **More than Two Generations.** Stand back and look at the document. How many generations are involved? If there are *more* than two generations, you can tell an invalidating story.

- **Classic Traps.** Does the contingency involve one of the classic traps? If so, then it's invalid. Many violations of the Rule fall into one of six classic traps. These are well known in the literature. Well-trained lawyers spot them on sight.

These guidelines don't cover all perpetuities problems. They are, however, a good start, along with their associated avoidance techniques.

D. Applying the Logic of the Rule

A degree of dogmatism . . . may be permitted here which would be unbecoming in other branches of the law.

—John Chipman Gray, The Rule Against
Perpetuities xi (4th ed. 1942)

How, then, do you prove one or the other? This is where the Rule takes on the feeling of a math puzzle.

The Rule is one of *logical proof.* Under the classic Rule, intent does not matter. Neither does good faith. The classical Rule is hard, definite, and cold. The Rule, John Chipman Gray tells us, should be "remorselessly applied."[54]

---

[54] John Chipman Gray, The Rule Against Perpetuities § 629, at 599 (4th ed. 1942).

Everything hinges on logical proof. Either the validating or invalidating side—one or the other—can be done. And once a proof is given, the game is over. Giving the proper proof is legal checkmate.

But how do you prove your case? Each side has its own logic. The validating side wins by pointing to a measuring life and showing the contingency must be resolved within that person's life plus 21 years.

In contrast, the invalidating side wins by telling an invalidating story. If it's possible the contingency won't be resolved within the perpetuities period, it's invalid.

E. Proving the Validating Side—Naming a Validating Life

To prove the validating side, you must name a person alive on the effective date and show, with certainty, the contingency will be resolved within their life plus 21 logical years. Again, the question is not whether the contingency will *happen*, but whether it will be *resolved*. Will we know—one way or the other—whether it will happen?

Here's an example. Assume a will has a gift to the testator's grandchildren who reach the age of 21. On the effective date of the will, the testator's death, only the testator's children can affect the contingency. Those children, in time, may produce grandchildren who reach the age of 21 or they may not. We don't know. But we do know we'll have an answer—one way or the other—within the lives of those children plus 21 years.

It doesn't matter whether the contingency itself is possible or likely. It could be bizarre or unlikely. Don't think about probabilities. All that matters is whether it'll be resolved.

F. Proving the Invalidating Side—the Perpetuities Storyline

To prove a violation of the Rule, a different proof is used. The method: you tell hypothetical stories about how, under certain conditions, the contingency "might not" be resolved within the period. Only one example is enough.

At first, you may think there are many stories, each dropping from the sky. But that's not so. There's only one story. And that one story is told again and again. Know that one story and you'll know them all.

Every violation of the Rule involves a standard storyline with three logical "moves." If all three moves can be made, the provision violates the Rule. Similarly, avoidance techniques stop the story from being told.

The critical first move always is this: assume a person who can affect the contingency is born after the effective date. This, of course, is just another way of saying the contingency is not limited to "lives in being."

Once that move is made, the other living people who could affect the contingency are removed (i.e., hypothetically killed off), and then we're left with a bare 21 years for resolution.

Now, let's see the basic story and the basic moves in action.

1. The Basic Invalidating Story

The basic invalidating story is a set formula with three moves:

- **Move 1—Person Born After Affecting the Contingency.** Assume a person who can affect the contingency, typically a child, is born after the effective date. Note: Because this person is born after the effective date, they cannot be a measuring life.

- **Move 2—Killing Off.** Assume everyone else alive on the effective date who can affect the contingency, typically parents and other children, are killed off. Note: This step eliminates all persons alive on the effective date who could affect the contingency.

- **Move 3—21 Years?** Then ask whether the contingency must be resolved within 21 years. Typically, it can't. The person born after the effective date cannot be a measuring life and all other persons alive on the effective date who could affect the contingency are killed off, so we're left with the 21-year period.

Here, the key is Move 1. If it can be made, then Move 2 is a given, and invalidity always follows. Thus, strategy focuses on Move 1. If it can be made, the provision violates the Rule. In contrast, many standard drafting tips work because, tactically, they block Move 1.

Remember, the story starts and ends with the facts on the effective date of the instrument. What actually happens after the effective date doesn't count.

2. Special Assumptions Available When Telling the Story

When telling the story, you're also free to make two unusual assumptions about life and death:

- **Universal Fecundity.** Any person alive on the effective date, regardless of age or gender, is capable of having children.

- **The Slaughter of the Innocents.**[55] Any number of persons alive on the effective date—regardless of age, health, or moral worthiness—can die together at any time.

In life, such assumptions may be remote, improbable, or even false. But they hold for the Rule against Perpetuities. Common sense, legal or otherwise, doesn't matter.

3. Logical Proof & However Remote

If there's any possibility the contingency may not resolved during the perpetuities period, it's invalid. The standard for the Rule is *however remote*. One invalidating scenario, however remote or unlikely, violates the Rule.

Casting probabilities away like this violates legal common sense. Here, even careful lawyers could violate the Rule. The result is a legal bullet in your document.

As important, here's what doesn't matter:

- What probably might happen after the effective date.

- What did, in fact, happen after the effective date.

- What any reasonable or cautious person might worry about.

Again, all that matters is what might happen, however remote.

G. Which Way to Jump—Revisited

Here, too, is another sticking point for law students new to the Rule. Remember this: the *only* way to validate a contingency is to name a measuring life. Here, "probably," or "almost certainly," or

---

[55] The term comes from Barton Leach. See W. Barton Leach, *Perpetuities: Staying the Slaughter of the Innocents*, 68 L.Q. Rev. 35 (1952).

even "all but one chance out of a billion" mean nothing. To win, the other side need only tell one invalidating story.

Once again, you're standing on the fence. If there's an invalidating story, you'll never have a measuring life. And if there's a measuring life, you'll never have an invalidating story.

This is where the rules of thumb come in:

- **Valid.** Ask whether Nottingham's Rule applies. If so, it's valid. The named person is the measuring life.

- **Invalid.** Ask whether it's more than two generations or whether it's a classic trap. If it meets either of these overlapping guidelines, it's invalid.

If you use these rules of thumb, you often can make the correct first guess and save time.

CHAPTER 12

Some Common Cases & Some Classic Traps

The Rule against Perpetuities . . . should be met early and often in such a way that students . . . learn to recognize the types of gifts which are likely to cause trouble.

—W. Barton Leach, *Property Law Taught in Two Packages*, 1 J. Legal Educ. 28, 56 (1948)

The Rule has many common, and simple, applications. It also has some classic traps. If you know just these, you'll know much of the Rule.

A. Some Common Applications of the Rule

They'll always be exotic or unusual applications of the Rule. That's part of its lore.

But most applications of the Rule are easy. Typically, they involve two things:

- Gifts to named persons.

- Gifts to children or grandchildren.

If you know just these, you'll how the Rule works in practice for the vast majority of estates.

You'll also see how gifts at death (i.e., wills and revocable trusts) have more options than lifetime gifts (i.e., irrevocable trusts).

Here are some common applications.

1. Named Persons & Nottingham's Rule

Think back to the *Duke of Norfolk's Case* and Nottingham's original rule: any contingency linked to a person alive on the effective date is valid. Why? Because the contingency is guaranteed to be resolved "within the compass" of that person's life.

The same rule still matters today. And it's useful for estate planning. It's broad and wide-ranging.

Note, in particular, the range of possible beneficiaries:

- Children or grandchildren (as in the *Duke of Norfolk's Case* itself).

- More distant relatives, or even friends, too.

- Any other living person.

Thus, under Nottingham's simple rule, just name the person and link the contingency. If done, the Rule is satisfied.

That's a good (and easy) rule to know.

2. Will or Revocable Trust—Gifts to Children

Most gifts are to children. Here, the Rule makes those easy.

Two options are possible. Both are simple. The bottom line: if mentioned, one way or another, children are covered.

Named Children & Nottingham's Rule—Any Gift. Any contingency linked to named children is covered. This, of course, was the original application of the Rule in the *Duke of Norfolk's Case*. The advantage here: different conditions could be used for different children.

Gifts to "Children" as a Group—Any Gift. But here's another interesting application. In the world of the Rule, open terms (like "children" or "grandchildren") often cause problems. Usually, it's because new members can be added after the effective date.

But not here. If the open term "children" is used, all the donor's children still are covered.

Why? For a will or revocable trust, the effective date is the death of the donor. At that point, of course, no more children can be conceived. "After-born" children, in short, are impossible.[1]

Thus, "children" is limited to people alive on the effective date. None can be added after. This means the children, as a group, can be validating lives. During their collective lifetimes, all contingencies will be resolved.

3. Will or Revocable Trust—Gifts to Grandchildren

Gifts to grandchildren aren't quite as easy. Grandchildren are the second generation. And treatment for them is different from children. Here, open terms can cause problems.

Named Grandchildren & Nottingham's Rule—Any Gift. For named grandchildren, any contingency linked to them is valid. Again, it's an easy application of Nottingham's Rule.

Gifts to "Grandchildren" as a Group—Limited Gifts. Here's where the extended common-law Rule matters. After Nottingham's original rule, courts eventually added an extra 21 years.

---

[1]   If you'd like to say "inconceivable" here, you can.

For grandchildren, this was a mixed blessing. On the one hand, this meant yet-to-be-conceived grandchildren could be gifted as well as existing grandchildren. It was a look into the future. On the other hand, it also caused problems for drafting.

The basic problem came down to classes. For children, there's only one class. And all children were in it. Any child, potentially, was a validating life. They need only be named (individually or collectively).

For grandchildren, though, it's different. While children can't be conceived after the death of the donor, grandchildren can. Significantly, under the Rule, this creates two different classes of "grandchildren," one on either side of the effective date:

- Grandchildren alive on the effective date.

- Grandchildren born after.

As a result, this limits gifts. Here's why:

- "Grandchildren," as a group, can't be validating lives. (The reason: some could be born after the effective date.)

- As a result, gifts to "grandchildren" are limited to "my grandchildren who reach the age of 21." Anything more violates the Rule.

4. Lessons for Wills & Revocable Trusts

In summary, here are basic lessons for wills and revocable trusts.

Gifts to Living People Are Easy. Nottingham's Rule still matters. Gifts to living beneficiaries are easy. Any linked condition is valid too. That always was the main idea behind the Rule. Here, this includes:

- Any named individual person.

- Donor's "children" as a group.

Gifts to Those "yet-to-Be-Born" Are Limited. Gifts to "yet-to-be-born" beneficiaries are limited.

- The only group covered: the donor's future grandchildren. No other later "yet-to-be-born" beneficiaries are valid.

- Plus, even here, conditions are limited. The only contingency allowed: reaching the age of 21.

5. Irrevocable Trust—Gifts to Children

Once we move to irrevocable trusts, even less can done.

An irrevocable trust adds a generation. Why? Because on the effective date—here the creation of the trust—the donor is still alive.

In turn, this moves possible beneficiaries up a generation. In short, what works for grandchildren in a will only works for children in an irrevocable trust.

Thus, while gifts to named children remain easy, those to "children" as a group become limited.

Gifts to Named Children—Nottingham's Rule. For named beneficiaries, any contingency involving them is valid. Unlike wills, however, this would not include gifts to "children" as a class.

Gifts to "Children" as a Group—Limited. Since the donor is still alive on the effective date, after-born children are possible. Thus, if the open term "children" is used, gifts must be limited to reaching the age of 21.

6. Irrevocable Trust—Gifts to Grandchildren

With an irrevocable trust, the settlor is still alive. Thus, after-born *children* are possible. This limits what can be done for grandchildren even more, since grandchildren are now the third generation. Again, relative to wills and revocable trusts, everything is pushed back a generation:

- Nottingham's Rule would cover gifts to named grandchildren.

- But any gift using the open term *grandchildren* would be invalid. This includes gifts at the age of 21.

7. Lessons for Irrevocable Trusts

In summary, here's what's possible for irrevocable trusts. Overall, Nottingham's Rule is dominant. Compared to wills and revocable trusts, however, everything else is more limited.

- **Gifts to Living People, Again, Are Easy.** Like wills, gifts to named people are easy. Here, though, it doesn't include gifts to "children" or "grandchildren" as a class.

- **Gifts to Those "yet-to-Be-Born" Are Even More Limited.** The only "yet-to-be-born" gifts possible are to children. And then only when they reach the age of 21. Gifts to future grandchildren or later generations aren't allowed.

B. Six Classic Traps

The Rule against Perpetuities has classic traps. All are famous. Some even have special names. A good lawyer knows them on sight.

Lawyers get caught because, on reflex, they fall back on the usual or probable. There are times when the Rule makes assumptions even careful lawyers miss.

Classic traps for the Rule fall into six categories:

- Age Contingencies in Excess of 21 Years.

- Gifts to the Grandchildren of a Person Now Alive.

- Irrevocable Trusts vs. Revocable Trusts or Wills.

- Fertile Octogenarian.

- Unborn Widow.

- Slothful Executor.

Some of the classic traps—Fertile Octogenarian, Unborn Widow, and Slothful Executor—are the work of Barton Leach.[2] The results themselves were not new. But Leach gave each a vivid and memorable name, and made them something special.

As used by Leach, they are, perhaps, the most famous characters ever put on legal stage. And they live only in the Land of Perpetuities. Once seen, they were hard to forget. It was a great teaching tool.

Leach used them for another purpose, too, and that was reform. If "that" can violate the Rule, Leach gently argued, maybe we should fix it.

Given all this, the Classic Traps matter for another reason, too. Because they are so famous and so memorable, mistakes about them are harder to forgive.

1. Age Contingencies in Excess of 21 [Three Generations]

Second-generation gifts must be resolved with 21 years. This could be gifts to grandchildren in a will, or gifts to children in an irrevocable trust. Thus, the Rule limits second-generation gifts more than first-generation gifts.

---

[2] W. Barton Leach, *Perpetuities in a Nutshell*, 51 Harv. L. Rev. 638, 643-46 (1938).

Here's the problem: donors may think gifts for grandchildren might be best at 25 or 30, or even later. After all, that's allowed for children. But the Rule doesn't allow ages greater than 21 for grandchildren (unless, of course, the grandchildren are named). In these settings, using ages greater than 21 violates the Rule. When you're at the limit, any extra takes you over. Barton Leach claimed "[s]uch gifts constitute the largest single group of invalid limitations."[3]

Example: Will or revocable trust. Assume A is the testator or settlor. Provision: "To my children, then to my grandchildren who reach the age of 25."

The Easy Assumption: Both my children and grandchildren are important. What I do for my children, I want to do for my grandchildren. And what I do for some, I want to do for all.

Story: This violates the Rule. Age limits in excess of 21 for grandchildren should be a red flag, unless it's a named person. Here's the standard storyline:

- **Move 1.** For example, assume on the effective date (i.e., A's death), A has one child, B. Then assume another grandchild, C, is born after the effective date.

- **Move 2.** Then assume B is killed less than four years after C is born.

- **Move 3.** The contingency is whether A would have a grandchild who reaches the age of 25. If B died less than 4 years after C was born, it cannot be determined within 21 years whether C will reach the age of 25.

---

[3]   Id. at 670.

Rationale: Any attempt to control three generations is invalid. Here, the first generation is lives in being and the second is the 21-year period. Using any number greater than 21 thus extends control into a third generation.

Other Variations: If the contingency was 30 years, then the Storyteller would say less than nine years after C was born. Similarly, if it was 22 years, then they would say less than one year after C was born. The result is the same.

Age of 21 vs. 21st Birthday: Even one extra day is invalid. Here's a famous example. Assume a gift in a will to a granddaughter. A gift to her "at the age of 21" complies with the Rule. But a gift to the same person "on her 21st birthday" doesn't. Why? Under an obscure common law doctrine, a person reached the age of 21 the first moment of the day *before* their 21st birthday. Barton Leach called this the Case of the Superannuated Minor.[4]

Avoidance Techniques: Following Nottingham's Rule, if A's will mentions a grandchild by name, then any age could be used. The age could be 21 or 25 or 95, or even 250. The named person is the validating life. This prevents the Storyteller from making Move 1.

This also illustrates a more general point: if open terms like "children" or "grandchildren" are used, the Storyteller can add members born after the effective date. In contrast, naming specific people blocks Move 1, and thus sets up an effective defense.

2. To the Grandchildren of a Person Now Alive [Three Generations]

A gift in a will or revocable trust to the donor's own grandchildren who reach the age of 21 is valid, and often used.

---

[4] W. Barton Leach, *The Careful Draftsman: Watch Out!* 47 ABA J. 259 (1961). As strict as this rule was, it did have one saving grace: it let people drink in bars one day sooner than they thought.

Thus, it's easy to assume a similar gift to the grandchildren of *other* people—say a living friend—is valid, too. But it's not.

Example: Will or revocable trust. Provision: "to the children of A for their lifetimes, then to the grandchildren of A who reach the age of 21." Assume A, a friend, is alive on the effective date.

The Easy Assumption: I like helping grandchildren. What I'm doing for my own, I'd like to do after my death for other relatives or friends.

Story: This violates the Rule. In effect, this tries to control three generations. A is the first generation, A's children are the second, and A's grandchildren are the third.

- **Move 1.** Assume a child, C, is born to A after the effective date of the instrument.

- **Move 2.** Then assume A dies, as well as any other children alive on the effective date.

- **Move 3.** Finally, assume C has a child (i.e., a grandchild of A) more than 21 years later.

Note: in contrast, if A is dead on the effective date of the instrument, the provision is valid, since only two generations are covered. In this case, A's children become the validating lives. We will know during their lives whether or not they have children.

Avoidance Techniques: List the existing grandchildren or children by name. Using the open term "grandchildren" allows the Storyteller to make Move 1 by assuming an after-born grandchild. Using named grandchildren stops the Storyteller from making Move 1.

3. *Irrevocable Trust vs. Revocable Trust or Will [Three Generations]*

What works in a revocable trust or will may not work in an irrevocable trust. Why? Different legal documents may have different effective dates. Using an irrevocable trust rather than a will or revocable trust changes the effective date. In effect, it *adds* a generation, since the settlor is still alive. Thus, rules move up a generation.

Example: Assume A is the settlor of an irrevocable trust. A provision gives a gift "to my grandchildren who reach the age of 21."

The Easy Assumption: A trust is a trust. If I can do it in one kind of trust, why can't I do in another? If it's good drafting for one kind of estate-planning document, it should be for another, too.

Story: This violates the Rule. This is three generations. It's another example of a gift to the grandchildren of a person now alive. Here's the story.

- **Move 1.** On the effective date, assume A has two children, B and C. Then assume another child, D, born after the effective date.

- **Move 2.** Then A, B, and C are killed.

- **Move 3.** Whether D, the after-born child, will have children who live to 21 won't be resolved within 21 years. For example, D could have a child 25 years later.

Rationale: The same provision in a will, of course, would be valid. But it's invalid in an irrevocable trust because the settlor's still alive. It's an attempt to control three generations rather than the usual two.

Avoidance Technique: Designate the grandchildren by name (e.g., "to my grandchildren B and C").

4. Fertile Octogenarian [Three Generation Variant]

This is a special—and famous—variant of the three-generation problem. It's based on *Jee v. Audley*, 29 Eng. Rep. 1186 (Ch. 1787).

As we've seen, gifts to the grandchildren of a person now alive violate the Rule (Classic Trap 2, previously). It's a classic attempt to control three generations. Violation follows once it's assumed, in Move 1, a child could be born after the effective date.

But what if, on similar facts, Move 1 couldn't be made? What if, in real life, A was 80 years old and incapable of having children? Could you argue it didn't violate the Rule?

Famously, under the Rule you can't. Every person—young or old, male or female—is assumed capable of having children. Age does not matter.

Example: Provision in a will that gives "life estate in A, then to the children of A, then to the grandchildren of A who reach the age of 21." Assume A is 80 years old and unable to have children.

The Easy Assumption: This person won't have more children. Everybody knows it's true. It's just a fact. And if there's anything lawyers care about, it's facts.

Story: This uses the standard story. But an irrebuttable—and false—assumption is used in Move 1.

- **Move 1.** The Rule conclusively presumes A can give birth after the effective date.

- **Move 2.** Then kill off A and all her other children and grandchildren alive on effective date.

- **Move 3.** A's imaginary after-born child will not reach the age of 21 in less than 21 years.

Rationale: While the result is often ridiculed, an argument can be made for the result. While giving birth is not possible at advanced age, adoption is. Thus, "after-born" may include "after-adopted."

The Rule vs. Standard Rationale: Below the surface, there are other arguments as well. First, if individual exceptions were allowed, where would it end? Questions about a fertile octogenarian may be easy, but questions about fertile sexagenarians (60s) or quinquagenarians (50s) may not. Neither may questions about birth control or vasectomies. Second, exceptions could only be made for living people. Litigation after death would be impractical. Third, answers to the Rule could no longer be given just by looking at the instrument itself.

Avoidance Techniques: Name the children or say "children now living who are then living."

5. *Unborn Widow [Three Generations]*

Gifts often are for children and grandchildren. But spouses of children may matter, too. For example, parents may want a widow or widower protected. But this simple idea has a famous trap as well.

Example: A bequest in trust to pay income "to my son, A, for life, then to my son's widow for life, then to Indiana University." Assume the son currently is married to B.

The Easy Assumption: The term "widow" was just a general way to describe the current spouse. That's obvious. Why else would we need a document drafted?

Story: "Widow" or "widower" are open terms. Thus, the following story could be told:

- **Move 1.** Under the logic of the Rule, the widow ultimately may be a person born after the effective date. While unlikely, because of the big age difference, it's still possible. Thus, assume B dies and then A marries C, a person born after the effective date.

- **Move 2.** Then kill off A, the son, leaving C as the widow.

- **Move 3.** Unborn widow, C, may die more than 21 years later. As a result, the interest to Indiana University doesn't vest until after the perpetuities period.

Rationale: Here drafters assume, reasonably, "widow" or "widower" refers to the present spouse. As an open term, however, it could include a later, yet-to-be-born spouse as well.

What's Invalid: What violates the Rule is the interest *after* the unborn widow. In the example above, it's the remainder to Indiana University. The interest of the unborn widow is valid. Why? It must vest within the life of A (the son), a life in being on the effective date.

Avoidance Techniques: Designate the widower or widow by name. This makes that person the measuring life.

6. *Administrative Contingency [No Named Persons]*

For a will, the effective date is the death of the testator. Sometimes, though, a donor may want to delay a gift for a short time after. This could be another trap.

Example: Gift in will "to A upon the distribution of my estate."

The Easy Assumption: It won't happen overnight, but everybody knows, one way or the other, it's going to happen. And soon enough, too. That's why we have a legal system.

Story: Under the relentless logic of the Rule, it's possible the administrative event may not happen within 21 years. While remote, it's possible the estate may be handled by what Barton Leach would call a Slothful Executor. There's no validating life here.

Other Examples: Other examples might include gifts "upon the probate of this will," "when a trust is formed," "when the gravel pits are exhausted," or "when the war ends."

Avoidance Techniques: Avoid administrative events. If used, link events to a person alive on the effective date. That will provide a measuring life.

C. Some Final Drafting Tips

In all these cases together—both the common applications and the Classic Traps—some guidelines emerge:

- **Nottingham's Rule.** It works. It also should be used more. Gifts for living persons need only name them to be valid.

- **Be Wary of Using Open Terms.** Open terms like "children," "grandchildren," and "widow" often cause problems. The reason: as open terms, they can include new members born after the effective date. Typically, too, it's not needed. Donors often mean only "lives in being" within those groups, but fail to limit it.

- **Gifts to Those yet Unborn.** Gifts to those yet unborn are limited. They can't be "lives in being." Only gifts to close relatives, such as future grandchildren, are possible. And even those covered are limited to reaching the age of 21.

All in all, just a small step beyond what happened in the *Duke of Norfolk's Case*.

CHAPTER 13

A Checklist, Some Problems, & Some Answers

Now's a good time to look back and summarize the Rule. First, let's work through a checklist for perpetuities problems. Once that's done, it's good to work through some problems. This should set the ideas in place.

A. An Approach to the Rule—a Checklist

Putting all this together gives the following approach to perpetuities problems. In all, there are five steps. If you think through each one, you'll be fine.

1. Type of Instrument

Look at the type of instrument involved (e.g., will, revocable trust, etc.). Based on this, determine the *effective date* of the instrument.

Remember the basic rules for effective dates:

• **Will.** Death of the testator.

- **Revocable Trust.** Death of the settlor.
- **Irrevocable Trust.** When the trust is executed.
- **Deed.** When the deed is executed.

This, of course, is when the perpetuities period starts.

Next, look at the type of contingency.

2. Nature of the Contingency

If no measuring lives are expressly identified (i.e., "name-your-own contingency"), locate the contingency in the document. Then, ask two questions:

- **What Must Happen?** What does the contingency require? Being born? Reaching a given age (e.g., 21 or 35?) Having a child? Going to the planet Mars?
- **Who Must Satisfy the Contingency?** A particular named person (i.e., Kari)? A member of an open group (i.e., "my grandchildren)? Any person?

3. Investigate: Who Is Alive, Who Is Dead?

After you isolate the contingency and know who can control the contingency, determine who is still alive on the effective date. Here, you may need to look outside the document. Ask questions and investigate. This may be beneficiaries or parents (or other relatives) of beneficiaries.

4. First Choice: Use the Rules of Thumb

Armed with this information, stand back and look at the contingency. Use the following rules of thumb:

- **Valid—Nottingham's Rule.** Does the contingency involve a named, living person? If so, it's valid.

- **Invalid—More than Two Generations.** Does the contingency involve more than two generations? If so, it's invalid.

- **Invalid—Classic Traps.** Does the contingency involve a class trap? Use the classic traps and their countermoves.

5. One Final Answer—Valid—Do the Proof— Name the Validating Life

If the contingency involves Nottingham's Rule or only two generations, you should have a validating life (or lives).

- Using the contingency, identify the relevant lives.

- Determine the relevant lives still alive on the effective date. Be prepared to look outside the instrument and investigate.

- A validating life will be found, if at all, among the relevant lives.

- **Do the Proof:** name the validating person (or persons) and give the proof.

6. Another Final Answer—Invalid—Do the Proof— Tell the Invalidating Story

If the contingency violates one of the rules of thumb, you should be able to tell an invaliding story and give the proof.

- Start with the effective date of the instrument and look forward.

- Consider what might happen, however remote.

- Ignore any facts that take place afterward.

- Use the special assumptions about fertility and death.

- **Do the Proof**: tell the invalidating story using the standard three-step storyline.

B. Some Perpetuities Problems

Each problem below first lists whether the instrument is a will, revocable trust, or irrevocable trust. It then lists a provision. Assume all named persons are alive, unless otherwise stated. For each, work the proofs.

Answers follow in the next section.

1. Will. To my first grandchild to reach the age of 21.

2. Irrevocable Inter Vivos Trust. To my first grandchild to reach the age of 21.

3. Will. To the first child of my granddaughter Ella to reach the age of 21.

4. Will. To the first child of my son Erick to graduate from law school.

5. Will. To the first child of my son Erick to reach the age of 25.

6. Will. To my son, Erick, for life, then to Erick's spouse, Alissa, for life, then the principal to be paid to the children of Erick then living.

7. Will. To such of my children and more remote issue as shall be living 21 years after the death of C, D, E, F, G, and H.

8. Will. To my granddaughter Nettie if she attends Indiana University.

9. Will. To my daughter Kari when my estate is probated.

10. Will. To the first child of my daughter Kari to reach the age of 25.

11. Will. To my daughter Kari if she reaches the age of 90.

12. Revocable Trust. To my granddaughter Lena if she reaches the age of 55.

13. Will. To the first of my children to reach the age of 30.

14. Inter Vivos Irrevocable Trust. To the first of my children to reach the age of 30.

15. Will. To the grandchildren of my friend A who reach the age of 21.

16. Will. To my grandchildren now alive who reach the age of 30.

17. Will. To the children of Ella living when my estate is probated.

18. Will. To Lena for life, then to Nettie if Nettie is living and, if not, then to Ella.

19. Revocable Trust. To such children of my brother Kevin who reach the age of 30. [Kevin is alive / Kevin is dead]

20. Will. To Ella, but if Nettie dies without issue during the life of Ella, then to Lena.

C. Some Perpetuities Answers

1.   Will. To my first grandchild to reach the age of 21.

Valid. The children of the testator are the validating lives.

Note: even if the testator doesn't yet have children when the will was executed, the contingency still will be resolved. The effective date is the death of the testator, not when the will is executed. On the effective date of the will—when the testator dies—the testator will either have children or not. Thus, we know the contingency will be resolved within the perpetuities period.

2.   Irrevocable Inter Vivos Trust. To my first grandchild to reach the age of 21.

Invalid. Three generations. Assume an after-born child. Then kill off the settlor and any children alive on the effective date. If so, then the after-born child may not have a child (e.g., my grandchild) who reaches 21 in less than 21 years.

Note: compare this with Problem 1 above. Same language, but different instruments. Because of different effective dates, there's a different result. Problem 1 is only two generations, while this Problem is three generations. It's all because of the shift from a revocable trust to an irrevocable inter vivos trust.

3.   Will. To the first child of my granddaughter Ella to reach the age of 21.

Valid. Nottingham's Rule. Ella is the validating life. Whether she has a child who reaches 21 is guaranteed to be resolved within 21 years of her death.

4. **Will. To the first child of my son Erick to graduate from law school.**

Invalid. Assume Erick has a child born after the effective date of the will. Then assume Erick and all his children alive on the effective date are killed off. If so, the after-born child may not graduate from law school within 21 years.

Note: the result would be the same even if, on the effective date, Erick had a child who was a third-year law student. Under the logic of the Rule, this child could die after the effective date and before graduation.

5. **Will. To the first child of my son, Erick, to reach the age of 25.**

Invalid. Three generations. Assume a child born after the effective date. Then assume Erick and any other children are killed off within less than four years. If so, then, contingency whether after-born child will live to 25 cannot be decided in 21 years.

6. **Will. To my son, Erick, for life, then to Erick's spouse, Alissa, for life, then the principal to be paid to the children of Erick then living.**

Valid. Potential unborn widow setting. But here the widow is named. Alissa is the validating life.

Note: if the open term *widow* is substituted for Alissa, the interest after is invalid. Remember, too, the invalid interest would be the one *after* the unborn widow dies. Here, it would be the gift to the children of Erick, including any after-born children.

7. Will. To such of my children and more remote issue as shall be living 21 years after the death of C, D, E, F, G, and H.

Valid. Validating lives can be named. This is a *name-your-own contingency*. Here, C, D, E, F, G, and H are expressly named as measuring lives. If reasonable in number, this satisfies the Rule. Plus you get 21 more years after their death. Depending on life expectancies and starting age of names persons, this could last well over 100 years.

8. Will. To my granddaughter Nettie if she attends Indiana University.

Valid. Nottingham's Rule. Will be resolved within Nettie's lifetime.

9. Will. To my daughter Kari when my estate is probated.

Invalid. Administrative contingency. Under the logic of the Rule, the estate may not be probated within 21 years.

10. Will. To the first child of my daughter Kari to reach the age of 25.

Invalid. Three generations. This is a gift to a grandchild after the age of 21. Assume an after-born child. Less than 4 years later, kill off Kari and all her children alive on effective date. If so, then whether an after-born child reaches 25 will not be resolved within 21 years.

11. Will. To my daughter Kari if she reaches the age of 90.

Valid. Nottingham's Rule. Named child. Kari is the validating life.

12. Revocable Trust. To my granddaughter Lena if she reaches the age of 55.

Valid. Nottingham's Rule, again. A named person is used. Lena is the validating life. Since this will be resolved within Lena's lifetime, any age is permitted.

Compare this example (grandchild) with Problem 11 (child). If it's a named person, it can be any generation. It also could be any relative, as well as any person alive on the planet.

13. Will. To the first of my children to reach the age of 30.

Valid. This is a first-generation gift. The children, collectively, are the validating lives. Because it is a will, there will be no after-born children.

14. Inter Vivos Irrevocable Trust. To the first of my children to reach the age of 30.

Invalid. An extra generation is added because of the irrevocable trust. Now there are three generations (settlor, children, then more than 21). Assume an after-born child. Then, kill off settlor and all children alive on effective date. If so, whether after-born child reaches the age of 30 will not be resolved within 21 years.

Note: compare with Problem 13. Both instruments use the same contingency. But the effective dates are different. What is valid in a will, may not be valid in an irrevocable inter vivos trust.

15. Will. To the grandchildren of my friend A who reach the age of 21.

Invalid. Three generations. The grandchildren of someone now alive. Assume an after-born child. Then kill of A and all A's children alive on the effective date. The after-born child now has less than 21 years to reach 21.

Note: the same gift to the testator's own grandchildren would be valid, since the effective date of will is the testator's death.

16. Will. To my grandchildren now alive who reach the age of 30.

Valid. Grandchildren now alive are the validating lives.

Note: the limitation to "now alive" stopped the first invalidating move and limited the class.

17. Will. To the children of Ella living when my estate is probated.

Invalid. Administrative contingency. A Slothful Executor may not probate the estate within 21 years.

But if changed to "children now living who are then living," those children would be validating lives.

18. Will. To Lena for life, then to Nettie if Nettie is living and, if not, then to Ella.

Valid. The contingency is whether Nettie is alive when Lena dies. This, in turn, will be decided within Nettie's life. Thus, Nettie is the validating life.

19. Revocable Trust. To such children of my brother Kevin who reach the age of 30. [Kevin is alive/Kevin is dead]

If Kevin is alive, this is invalid. Three generations. The grandchildren of someone now alive. Assume an after-born child. Then kill off Kevin and all his children alive on effective date. Then after-born child can't reach 30 in less than 21 years.

If Kevin is dead, the contingency is valid. The validating lives are the children of Kevin.

20. Will. To Ella, but if Nettie dies without issue during the life of Ella, then to Lena.

Valid. The facts of the *Duke of Norfolk's Case*. By now, this should be easy. The validating life is Nettie. And, of course, Nottingham's Rule.

CHAPTER 14

A Perpetuities Miscellany—Some Advanced Topics

The Rule has many applications. Not all, though, are critical to understanding the basic Rule. If this is your first time through, feel free to skip this chapter. At the same time, once you've finished the basics, feel free to come back. It's good to know some of the other twists and special applications of the Rule.

Four advanced topics will be covered:

- Charities.

- Powers of Appointment.

- Class Gifts.

- Saving Clauses.

In addition, so will two other *how long* rules:

- The Rule against Accumulation of Income.

- The Rule against Suspension of the Power of Alienation.

A. Public Charities & the Rule

Charities get special treatment under the Rule. The main reason: alienability is not an issue for public charities. Once created, charitable gifts cannot be destroyed by the government.[1] Plus, unlike private trusts, charities cannot be terminated by beneficiaries. They remain inalienable and indestructible interests.

Thus, the common-law Rule against Perpetuities does not apply to charitable trusts. Instead, charitable trusts can continue forever.[2] This encourages gifts. It also maximizes public benefit. Here, perpetuities are good.

B. Gifts Over—the Charity-to-Charity Exception

So-called "gifts over" also may involve charities. But not all of them are protected under the Rule.

Imagine the following executory interest between two private persons:

To A but if alcohol is ever served on the premises, then to B.

Here, title could shift centuries later. This is a clear case of contingent title. Plus, A has little incentive to invest.

If both A and B are charities, however, the Rule against Perpetuities doesn't apply. Here's an example:

To Charity A but if alcohol is ever served on the premises, then to Charity B.

Even after the shift, title remains in the public. And the property keeps serving the public.

---

[1]   *Dartmouth College v. Woodward*, 17 U.S. 518 (1819).

[2]   Restatement (Second) of Trusts § 365 (1959).

For the exception to apply, however, *both* parties must be charities. If either party is a private person, it violates the Rule. Thus, both of these examples violate the Rule:

> To A, but if alcohol is ever sold on the premises, then to Charity B.

> To Charity A, but if alcohol is ever sold on the premises, then to B.

The traditional charity-to-charity exception for gifts over is codified in the Uniform Statutory Rule Against Perpetuities. USRAP § 4(5).

C. Powers of Appointment

The power of appointment is the most efficient dispositive device that the ingenuity of Anglo-American lawyers has ever worked out.

—W. Barton Leach, *Powers of Appointment,*
24 ABA J. 807, 807 (1938)

1. What Powers Are

It all starts with contingencies. Typically, donors must make plans—as the Earl of Arundel did—while still alive. If not, then the time is past.

But what if you could wait a generation, instead? What if you could delegate final disposition of property to another person, after your death? This way, someone else alive then could make the decision based on people and circumstances a generation later?

That, in essence, is a power of appointment.

2. Types of Powers

In General. Powers are varied, flexible, and powerful. Different groups, alternatives, and presumptions are possible.

Option sets abound. Powers could be exercised later in a will. They also could be exercised while living.

The Powers of Powers of Appointment. Powers aren't limited to a single decision. Powers also can create other powers, or even trusts. This gives them great flexibility.

3. General Powers vs. Special Powers

Today, the most important distinction is between general and special powers of appointment. Here's the difference:

- **General.** If the holder of the power is included on the list of possible donees, it's a general power. In essence, that person can make the property their own.

- **Special.** In contrast, if the holder only can appoint to others, it's a special power of appointment.

Why does this matter? For purposes of federal estate tax, general powers are included in the estate of the holder. The government considers this ownership enough to include in a person's estate.

4. Why Powers Matter for the Rule

Contingencies still exist. Here, though, they're not contingencies about outside facts, such as "would Thomas die without issue?" Instead, the key here is the decision by the holder.

5. Applying the Rule—General Powers

A general power is considered owned by the donee. Thus, it's just about the Rule, fresh, going forward.

In turn, validity for general powers turns on two questions:

- **Validity of Power Itself.** Is the power held by a valid person? The critical question: is the person holding the power *alive* on the effective date of the instrument? If so, the power's valid. On the other hand, if the power's given to a person yet unborn, it's invalid.

- **Validity of Exercise.** Since it's a general power, it's treated as if the holder owned the property. Thus, the period starts when the power itself is exercised.

6. Applying the Rule—General Testamentary Powers & Special Powers

For special powers, in contrast, the holder is viewed as the agent of the donor. Here, the holder doesn't own the property, but acts only as later agent for the donor.

Here, agency has advantages. The donor first sets general guidelines for the contingency. Later—with updated facts—the agent picks the particular contingency to use. Until it's made, though, ultimate title is contingent.

Validity of Power Itself. As, in essence, the choice of the *donor*, the question is this: is it possible the power may be exercised *after* the perpetuities period? If, on the effective date of the instrument, the person is alive, the power is valid. If unborn, then it's invalid.

Validity of Exercise. The perpetuities period here starts when the power is created. Why? Because it's viewed, ultimately, as the choice of the donor. Now, though, there's an extra twist: when the power's created, we don't know the final contingency. We may know the general range of options possible. But we won't know the final answer until it's picked, perhaps much later, by the donee.

Second-Look Doctrine. To apply the Rule here, therefore, the donee's choice after the fact must be read *back into* the original power. Once done, the regular Rule is applied. This is known as the *second-look doctrine*.

D. Class Gifts[3]

For class gifts, the Rule has an infamous standard—its *all-or-nothing* rule. To understand it, you first must understand class gifts. Once done, you can see how the Rule applies.

1. The Nature of Class Gifts—Gifts to Individuals vs. Gifts to Groups

Often gifts are to individual people, such as "my granddaughter, Nettie." This could be to several people, too, so long as each person is named. An example would be "to my granddaughters, Nettie, Ella, and Lena."

But gifts also can be to *groups* of people. For example, I might give gifts to "my grandchildren," "my siblings," or "my heirs." On the other hand, a term without clear legal boundaries—like "my friends"—would not qualify.

2. Size of Groups & Basic Math

By nature, groups can vary in size. The group consisting of "my grandchildren" could be three or thirty people. And for certain kinds of gifts, that matters.

If I want to give $10,000 to *each* grandchild—what is known as gifts of *specific sums* or per capita gifts—then $10,000 is counted out to each grandchild, however many there may be. The math is easy.

---

[3] See Restatement (Third) of Property: Wills & Other Donative Transfers §§ 13.1, 15.1 (2011).

Other times, though, it may not be. Assume, instead, I want $10,000 to be *shared* by the group. Here, basic math enters the picture.

Before the money can be counted out, the number of grandchildren must be known. Think of this as the *denominator* problem. Before we can divvy up the $10,000, we need to know the number of pieces. Will it be three or thirty? What will the number be?

3. Class Openings & Closings

In short, we can't do the math until the class closes. A class is closed when no one else can be added. This gives us the maximum number. Once known, a first division can be made.

Class gifts close in one of two ways. First, a group may close *physiologically.* For example, assume a gift "to the children of A." But also assume A is dead when the gift is given. Here, A can't add children to the class. Thus, the group is physiologically closed. Now, the math can be done.

But what, instead, if A is alive on the date of the gift? Now, more children can be born. Thus, the group is not physiologically closed. How, then, is the group closed?

Here, the common law provides a special rule—*the rule of convenience.* In essence, under this rule, the class closes when the first member can take. Once closed, no one else can be added to the class.

4. Applying the Rule to Class Gifts—Generally

Applying the Rule to class gifts involves two steps. First, when does the class close? This could be physiologically or by the rule of convenience. Once done, this identifies the relevant members of the group. Second, all interests in that group must be resolved within the perpetuities period.

5. Applying the Rule to Class Gifts—All-or-Nothing

Now things get interesting. It all gets down to a fine point: *when* are class gifts resolved? In particular, what if some contingencies in the group are resolved during the perpetuities period, but others aren't?

Here, in theory, two options could be imagined.

- **Members Already Resolved Are Saved.** One option: apply the Rule on a person-by-person basis. If the member meets the contingency, it's valid; if they don't, it's not. Then, only strike the invalid gifts, leaving the rest.

- **No One Safe Until All Are Resolved.** Another option is group-based. Here, it's the group *as* a group. They stand or fall together. Unless all members are safe, no one is safe.

The common-law Rule takes the second option. Under the Rule against Perpetuities, class gifts are governed by the *all-or-nothing* rule of *Leake v. Robinson*, 35 Eng. Rep. 979 (Ch. 1817). A class gift is either completely valid or completely invalid.

6. An Example of All-or-Nothing[4]

Here's an example:

To A for life, then to A's children for life, then to A's grandchildren who reach the age of 25.

---

[4] A classic piece explaining and then criticizing this rule is W. Barton Leach, *The Rule Against Perpetuities and Gifts to Classes*, 51 Harv. L. Rev. 1329 (1938).

This is a classic three-generation problem. Assume A is alive on the effective date. Assume, too, there are two grandchildren, B and C, alive on the effective date. Assume B is 24 years old and C is 21.

Since both B and C are alive on the effective date, their fate will be resolved within the perpetuities period. If that's all it took, the class gift—at least to them—would be valid. But *other* grandchildren, of course, could be born after. And this would apply whether or not A is capable of having children, thanks to *Jee v. Audley* and its conclusive assumption of fertility. Thus, for any after-born children, the gift would be invalid.

Here's where the all-or-nothing rule of *Leake v. Robinson* hits home. Rather than applying the Rule grandchild-by-grandchild (as B and C might want), it's applied all-or-nothing to the entire group. Unless the gift is valid for all the other possible grandchildren, too, both B and C lose out.

E. Saving Clause—Self-Help for Lawyers

A saving clause is now a standard part of practice. There's no reason not to use one.

In effect, a saving clause[5] is a self-executing reform by the lawyer drafting the will or trust. The thought: "If, by chance, I've violated the Rule, I'll draft—as backup—another contingency of my own making to guarantee my client's contingency ends within the perpetuities period."

1. Saving Clause—How It Works

A saving clause prevents violations from happening in the first place. Thus, the clause will *save* the contingency from challenge and termination. Once done, too, there's no need for reforms. This is just another example of *name-your-own contingency*. Instead of

---

[5]   A usage note: it's *saving*, as in protect, not *savings*, as in banks.

serving as the primary measure, however, it serves as backup. In effect, it adds a second, but guaranteed, contingency.

2. *Saving Clause—Contents*

The saving clause needs to do two things:

- **Termination Clause.** Say when the trust terminates. The measuring lives used may, but need not be, related to the main contingency. A key point: limit the named persons, whoever they are, to ones *living* on the effective date of the instrument. Often, beneficiaries are used.

- **Disposition Clause.** As important, say what happens after. Here, it's important that the disposition be similar to the main instrument. If for a will, for example, it could be "to my then living descendants, per stirpes" or, if a trust, "to the persons entitled to income in the same proportion as their shares." This way, the full intent of the donor survives.

Both parts are needed. A saving clause has both.

3. *Saving Clause—an Example*

Here's an example from Elvis Presley's will. First, here's the termination clause:

> Having in mind the rule against perpetuities, I direct that . . . each trust created under this will . . . shall end, unless sooner terminated under other provisions of this will, twenty-one (21) years after the death of the last survivor of such of the beneficiaries hereunder as are living at the time of my death;

And, as it continues, here's the disposition clause:

> [A]nd thereupon that the property held in trust shall be distributed free of all trust to the persons then entitled to receive the income or principal therefrom, in the proportion in which they are then entitled to receive such income.

At the same time, no single boilerplate will work for every gift. Instead, it must be tailored to the contingencies of each gift. As one example, because of different effective dates, language drafted for a will may not work for an irrevocable trust.

F. Other "How Long" Rules

The Rule against Perpetuities limits how long contingencies may be unresolved. But other *how long* rules may apply to trusts as well.

1. The Rule Against Accumulation of Income

One is the *rule against accumulation of income*. This governs how long money can accumulate in a trust without being paid out. The rule was a response to an eccentric request in the 1797 will of Peter Thellusson, a wealthy merchant.

Unlike the usual parent who wanted to provide for children and grandchildren, Thellusson did something else: he wanted no money paid to them at all. Instead, he wanted his money accumulated for three generations—his children, grandchildren, and great-grandchildren. Only then would it be paid to his then living descendants. As Barton Leach described it, "Peter Thellusson thus locked his treasure in a mausoleum and flung the key to some remote descendent yet unborn."[6]

---

[6]   J.H.C. Morris & W. Barton Leach, The Rule Against Perpetuities 267 (2d ed. 1962).

After extensive litigation, the House of Lords decided, in *Thellusson v. Woodford*,[7] there was no limit on accumulations other than the Rule against Perpetuities.

The case caused a stir. Some saw it as caprice or spite. Others saw wasted resources. In response, Parliament passed a law, the Accumulations Act[8] (also known called the "Thellusson Act"). This limited accumulations to various periods short of the Rule.

In the United States, most states with a rule against accumulations in private trusts use the same period as the Rule against Perpetuities.

2. An American Twist—Wellington Burt

While it did not involve the rule against accumulation of income, there's an interesting analog to *Thellusson* in American law. It's worth knowing, all by itself.

While most donors favor children and grandchildren, not all do. A classic example comes from the will of Wellington Burt, a lumber baron from Wisconsin.

When Wellington Burt died in 1919, he was one of the richest persons in America. His fortune was estimated between $60-90 million (worth about $1 billion today).

Angry at his children and grandchildren, he played the miser. Burt gave his children modest annual allowances, similar to what he left his cook, housekeeper, and other servants.

The bulk of his estate, however, was withheld. He decided— out of spite—it would be paid out only 21 years after all his living children and grandchildren were dead. That took 91 years. Eventually, in 2011, various descendants, all unborn at Burt's death,

---

7   32 Eng. Rep. 1030 (Ch. 1805).
8   39 & 40 Geo. III c. 98 (1800).

split $100 million. Litigation and lawyer fees significantly lowered the final amount.

3. Rule Against Suspension of the Power of Alienation

Ultimately, the Rule against Perpetuities promotes alienation of property. Markets should work. Otherwise, society is harmed. Under the Rule, families get to control property but then, after a while, markets apply again.

The common law, however, has many rules about property and alienation. The Rule against Perpetuities isn't the only one.

A related one is the rule against suspension of the power of alienation. Here's the relationship between the two:

- **Rule Against Suspension of the Power of Alienation.** This applies to present interests. The basic purpose: guarantee present property interests can be bought and sold. This promotes the highest and best use of property. It also promotes overall social prosperity. This rule applies to both commercial and private settings.

- **Rule Against Perpetuities.** This applies only to future interests. The basic purpose: prevent donors from using contingencies to keep property within the family (and thus off the market) for excessive periods of time. The typical setting is donative gifts within the family.

One important bit of perpetuities trivia: before John Chipman Gray came along, the two rules often were conflated. Even Gray confessed he made the same mistake at first, too.[9] But, once made,

---

[9]   John Chipman Gray, The Rule Against Perpetuities xi n.3 (4th ed, 1942) (preface to first edition).

the distinction became key to his treatment of the Rule as one, exclusively, about future interests.

In turn, Gray was always clear about the distinction:

- He drew attention to the two different rules, repeatedly, in his famous treatise.[10]

- He wrote a different book on restraints on present interests.[11]

Gray thus played a critical role in distinguishing the two.

Unfortunately, before Gray's treatise, some states passed legislation—supposedly about perpetuities—that focused instead on suspending the power of alienation. As a result, some states passed statutes limiting suspension of alienation for the perpetuities period.[12]

---

[10] Id. § 2.1, at 4, § 119.

[11] John Chipman Gray, Restraints on the Alienation of Property (2d ed. 1895).

[12] Restatement (Third) of Property: Wills & Other Donative Transfers, Chapter 27, Reporter's Note 575 n.2 (2011).

PART 5

Modern Reform of the Common-Law Rule

CHAPTER 15

An Interlude—
Personalities—
Barton Leach

A. Barton Leach & Gray's Rule

In 1965, Barton Leach described the Rule against Perpetuities as a "pedestrian, often somnolent, area of property law."[1] That was about to change. And he would have a lot to do with it.

In 1938, Leach wrote *Perpetuities in a Nutshell*, a classic law review article.[2] In it, he summarized Gray's 700-page treatise in 35 pages. It was an instant classic for law students. Walk into any law library in America today, pick out the volume for Leach's piece, and it will fall open to his article, touched by thousands of hands.

More than any other professor in America, the common-law Rule was his. Leach named the classic traps, all in his crisp way. Among others, he named the Unborn Widow, the Slothful Executor, and, most famously, the Fertile Octogenarian.[3] He also labeled the

---

[1]   W. Barton Leach, *Perpetuities: The Nutshell Revisited*, 78 Harv. L Rev. 973, 978 (1965).

[2]   W. Barton Leach, *Perpetuities in a Nutshell*, 51 Harv. L. Rev. 638 (1938).

[3]   Id. at 643-46.

Magic Gravel Pit and the Precocious Toddler.[4] The labels still are used today.

B. Leach's Change of Heart

By the 1950s, though, Leach had a change of heart. His views about Gray and the Rule had changed. "[G]reat men and their great books create problems," argued Leach, "They tend to freeze things in antique patterns."[5] The Rule he knew so well needed updating.

And Leach acted on it. A nimble and engaging writer, Leach was a consummate raconteur. He brought his story-telling skills to bear on reforming the Rule. He used vivid and gripping titles, decrying the Rule's "slaughter of the innocents,"[6] and its "reign of terror."[7]

Proclaiming the Rule less than perfectly understood by lawyers or judges, Leach traveled the country.[8] He consulted with legislators and lawyers, both in the United States and England.

In his quest for reform, Leach wrote article after article in bar journals and law reviews. He drafted legislation and applauded reforms. He also co-wrote a book on the Rule and its reforms.[9]

C. Barton Leach as Progenitor of Reform

For the first time, Barton Leach put reform of Gray's Rule into play. Leach gave us two classic options:

---

[4]   W. Barton Leach, *Perpetuities in Perspective: Ending the Rule's Reign of Terror*, 65 Harv. L. Rev 721, 731-34 (1952)

[5]   W. Barton Leach, supra note 1, at 973.

[6]   W. Barton Leach, *Perpetuities: Staying the Slaughter of the Innocents*, 68 L.Q. Rev. 35 (1952).

[7]   W. Barton Leach, supra note 4.

[8]   He even made it to Indiana, as guest of the state bar. See W. Barton Leach, *The Rule Against Perpetuities and the Indiana Perpetuities Statute*, 15 Ind. L.J. 261 (1940). We were glad.

[9]   J.H.C. Morris & W. Barton Leach, The Rule Against Perpetuities (2d ed. 1962).

- Reformation.

- Wait-and-See.

When Leach died in 1971, few states had adopted either reform. Through Leach's efforts, though, reformation and wait-and-see became set points in law school casebooks. Every law student knew them. So did every professor who taught Property or Wills & Trusts.

The modern era of statutory reform of the Rule starts in 1986 with the Uniform Statutory Rule Against Perpetuities (USRAP). It's also been the most successful. As we'll see, USRAP starts with Gray's Rule and then adds both wait-and-see and reformation. The other modern reform, the two full generation model of the *Restatement (Third) of Property*, uses wait-and-see and reformation as well.

Walter Barton Leach would have been pleased.

CHAPTER 16

Reforms Generally—
Reformation &
Wait-and-See

A. Reform of the Rule—an Introduction—the Meaning of Reform

Significantly, modern reform for the Rule is not about abolishing the Rule or changing its policies. Instead, it's about something else—fixing violations of the Rule.

For law, this is a different type of reform. Here, it's about wanting the Rule to apply even if lawyers first make mistakes.

The goal: make compliance with the Rule universal. This keeps the Rule in place and helps lawyers use it for clients.

Before looking at the details of major statutory reform today, however, it's important to look at two important types of reform:[1]

---

[1] Another and earlier reform was *specific statutory repair*. The idea was simple: fix, by statute, some of the classic mistakes, such as the Fertile Octogenarian. A few famous errors were cut off at the top. But the rest of Gray's Rule remained intact. Thus, if the mistake wasn't on the statutory list, there was no relief. This is covered well in Lawrence W. Waggoner, *Perpetuity Reform*, 82 Michigan L. Rev. 1718, 1728-50 (1983).

- **Reformation.** This is broad reform. If Gray's Rule is violated, this allows a court to fix the mistake.

- **Wait-and-See.** This also is broad reform. If the Rule is violated, this looks to whether the contingency was, in fact, later resolved.

Both reformation and wait-and-see offer cures for violations of Gray's Rule. Both, too, are key parts of perpetuities law today.

After this introduction, the next chapter looks at the most widely-adopted modern statutory reform—the Uniform Statutory Rule Against Perpetuities—as well as the recent two-generation reform from the *Restatement (Third) of Property*. Both make significant use of reformation and wait-and-see.

B. Major Reform—Reformation

No lawyer wants to violate the Rule. It's a mistake and, traditionally, the consequences were severe. Not only was the estate plan spoiled, but the lawyer could face malpractice.

Elsewhere in the law, of course, lawyers could make mistakes, too. For example, both parties may have overlooked an error of description in a deed. When it happened elsewhere, though, the standard legal cure was *reformation*. Using its equitable powers, a court could change the document to conform to the actual intent of the parties.[2]

If so easy elsewhere, why was reformation at first an unused remedy with the Rule? Here, as we'll see, Gray and formalism played a critical role.

---

[2]   John H. Langbein & Lawrence W. Waggoner, *Reformation of Wills on the Ground of Mistake: Change of Direction in American Law?* 130 U. Pa. L. Rev. 521, 524–28, 546-49 (1982).

1. The Rule as Math

For Gray, the Rule was math. It had right and wrong answers:

[I]f a decision agrees with [the Rule], it is right; it if does not agree with it, it is wrong. In no part of the law is the reasoning so mathematical in its character: none has so small a human element.[3]

Thus, in Gray's formalistic world, intent didn't matter. For Gray, the Rule was one of law, not construction. It had sums and right answers. As Gray proudly stated, up front, in the Preface to his first edition in 1886, there was no human excuse for mistakes:

If the answer to a problem does not square with the multiplication table one may call it wrong, although it be the work of Sir Isaac Newton.[4]

In short, if your sums were wrong, it didn't matter if you meant for them to be right. Thus, for Gray, the Rule was "intended to defeat intention."[5]

2. John Chipman Gray on Reformation

Thus, for Gray, reformation was just flat-out wrong. It had no place in the world of perpetuities.

Gray didn't hesitate to make his considerable opinion known, either. In 1891, the Supreme Court of New Hampshire, in *Edgerly v. Barker*, 66 N.H. 434, 31 A. 900 (1891), did exactly what Gray said it shouldn't do—it reformed a will to prevent a grandfather from disinheriting his grandchildren.

---

[3] John Chipman Gray, The Rule Against Perpetuities xi (4th ed. 1942).
[4] Id.
[5] Id. at 762.

Gray was nothing short of apoplectic. He added a special 14-page appendix to his treatise to voice his disapproval.[6] After calling it "contrary to every previous case,"[7] Gray was blunt: "It is a dangerous thing to make such a radical change in a part of the law which is concatenated with almost mathematical precision."[8]

So much for reformation.

3. Leach's Role in Reformation

Thus, when Barton Leach first proposed reformation in the 1950s and 1960s, it was more radical than it seems today. In truth, he was directly challenging Gray.

To his credit, Leach presented reformation as a modest and natural choice. He calmly encouraged courts to accept *Edgerly v. Barker* as precedent, and he asked states for general legislation allowing reformation.[9]

4. Benefits & Costs of Reformation

Again, reformation does not change the Rule. Instead, it changes the document to comply with the Rule. Rather than being struck down, the gift is reformed. The policies of the Rule remain in place.

While reformation can fix the error, it has costs, too. Reformation requires litigation, lawyers, and courts. It also takes time and money.

But those costs yield significant benefits:

- The intent of the donor is upheld.

---

[6] Id. at 752-66 (Appendix G).

[7] Id. at 752.

[8] Id. at 757.

[9] W. Barton Leach, *Perpetuities in Perspective: Ending the Rule's Reign of Terror*, 65 Harv. L. Rev. 721, 746-48 (1952).

- A challenge to the gift is forestalled.

- Malpractice claims are reduced.

5. Reformation as Remedy

In response to Leach, a few courts and legislatures openly adopted reformation as an option. Overall, however, it had limited adoption during Leach's life.

At the same time, Leach made reformation a respectable legal option. With adoption of the Uniform Statutory Rule Against Perpetuities (USRAP) in 1986, reformation finally gained widespread acceptance.

C. Major Reform—Wait-and-See

While reformation is a general remedy used in other areas of law, the second major reform, *wait-and-see*, is specific to perpetuities. It's not used elsewhere.

The idea of *wait-and-see* comes from the startling mismatch, at times, between the *however remote* standard of Gray's Rule and real life events. Critics of the Rule, particularly Barton Leach, often highlighted classic traps, such as the Fertile Octogenarian, the Unborn Widow, and the Slothful Executor.

Using Gray's math, each violated the Rule. Yet, each violation also seemed innately unfair. In each case, the Rule used some highly improbable, if not outright false, assumption about *what might happen*. Why let one hypothetical grain of chance, in an entire universe, strike down a donor's gift?

If judged, instead, by *actual* rather than *hypothetical* events, each becomes easy. If we used actual events instead, the Rule better reflects real life. The 80-year-old does not have a child, the widow is not unborn, and the estate is promptly probated. Waiting gives new answers.

1. The Pennsylvania Statute

In 1947, the Pennsylvania legislature passed a one-sentence statute. Contingencies no longer would be tested by *what-might-happen*. Now, it would be what *actually* happened, instead:

> Upon the expiration of the period allowed by the common law rule against perpetuities as measured by actual rather than possible events any interest not then vested and any interest in members of a class the membership of which is then subject to increase shall be void.[10]

Calling the approach *wait-and-see*, Barton Leach sang its praises. He urged states to adopt wait-and-see along with reformation, so each could be used.[11]

2. The Workings of Wait-and-See

Leach's classic traps may have been the genesis for wait-and-see. But it's important to see how wait-and-see works. Under Gray's Rule, the classic traps did not have validating lives. That's why they violated the Rule. Wait-and-see doesn't change that.

Instead, wait-and-see works by giving a second chance for validation. Rather than striking it down, we wait and see whether the contingency's resolved by later events. At the same time, the classic invalidating story—with its *however remote* assumption—is removed. Thus, everything now turns on real life events.

---

[10] 20 Pa. Cons. Stat. Ann. § 6104(b) (2017). After 2007, Pennsylvania allowed perpetuities for 360 years. 20 Pa. Cons. Stat. Ann. § 6107.1 (2017). It's good Barton Leach did not live to see his famous wait-and-see statute discarded for the perpetuities of old. Walter Barton Leach, I have no doubt, would have cried.

[11] W. Barton Leach, *Perpetuities: What Legislatures, Courts, and Practitioners Can Do about the Follies of the Rule*, 13 Kansas L. Rev. 351, 357-58 (1965).

3. Wait-and-See—Classic Cases & Others— Flipping the Odds

Now, with wait-and-see, probabilities are flipped. Before, "only one" in a billion could strike something down. Now, instead, we can safely wait for "all but one" in a billion to play out. With new probabilities, contingencies are easily resolved with time.

The problem before: contingencies could be struck down on odds so low that no reasonable person would think them possible. Now, in contrast, it's a benefit. We can plan on it happening.

Once measured by *actual* rather than *hypothetical* events, many of Leach's classic traps are solved. The Fertile Octogenarian is the easiest. We know—for certain and every time—how it will be resolved: the octogenarian never has children. Thus, the contingency always will be valid.

The Unborn Widow is similar. Unlike the Fertile Octogenarian, we can't say it will never happen. Still, the probabilities are compelling. The same goes for any administrative contingency. It's highly unlikely any task will be delayed as long as the Rule assumes. Practicing lawyers are not Slothful Executors.

Once past the classic traps, however, results may be less certain. Assume, for example, a gift in a will "to my grandchildren who reach the age of 40." Here, actual events may not be as easy to predict.

4. Wait-and-See—How Long We Wait

For wait-and-see to work as total reform, therefore, other questions need to be resolved. Most important, exactly *how long* do we wait? No one answer was obvious. Yet without one, wait-and-see could not work. A variety of different "waits" were proposed. Of them, two were the most important:

- **Set Period of Years.** Here, use the same set period—say 90 or 120 years—for everyone. Often this tries, in a general way, to approximate the perpetuities period.

- **Causal Lives.** Use the actual lives of people who could affect the contingency. In essence, this is a case-by-case standard, using the contingency in each document. This view is associated with Professor Jesse Dukeminier, its leading proponent.[12] This also appears to be what Barton Leach intended.

5. What We Do While We're Waiting

The turn to what actually happens also means real people and real events must be found, followed, tracked, and watched. Without it, we won't know whether contingencies are resolved. This adds some administrative costs to the initial mistake.

6. Benefits of Wait-and-See

Wait-and-see only matters for mistakes. If done right under Gray's Rule, there's no need to wait. We know, instantly, from the words on the page.

But, if a mistake is made, wait-and-see saves the gift. It also upholds the basic policy of the Rule. Wait-and-see doesn't change the basic Rule. Instead, it just changes how the Rule itself is applied.

For lawyers and donors, wait-and-see gives the same general benefits as reformation. We start with these:

- The intent of the donor is upheld.

---

[12] See Jesse Dukeminier, *Perpetuities: The Measuring Lives*, 85 Colum. L. Rev. 1648 (1985).

- A challenge to the gift is forestalled.

- Malpractice claims are reduced.

All mistakes of the Rule have costs. For reformation, there's immediate litigation. Wait-and-see, though, has different costs— events after must be tracked, both people and events. Plus, if events are not resolved in time, reformation may be needed later as well.

7. Adoption of Wait-and-See

When Leach died in 1971, only a few states had adopted wait-and-see by court decision or legislation. But it was a start.

Later, the banner of wait-and-see was picked up by Professor James Casner, one of Leach's colleagues at Harvard. Casner later became the Reporter for the *Restatement (Second) of Property*. After vigorous debate, Casner wrote wait-and-see into the Restatement in 1983.[13] Few states, however, adopted it.

Passage of the Uniform Statutory Rule Against Perpetuities (USRAP) in 1986 finally brought wait-and-see into widespread use. Wait-and-see also plays prominently in the most recent perpetuity reform offered by the *Restatement (Third) of Property*. Thus, wait-and-see remains the centerpiece of perpetuities reform today.

D. The Remedies—Alone or Combined

A final (and unusual) part of perpetuities reform is this: it's not about choosing between reformation or wait-and-see, as if they were competing options. That's not the idea.

Instead, it's about using both remedies together. It's their combined power that matters. It's important, too, to see how they work together. There's a logic to their order.

---

[13] Restatement (Second) of Property: Donative Transfers § 1.4 (1983).

1. The Order of Remedies—First Wait-and-See, Then Reformation

While wait-and-see and reformation work together, they follow a predictable order: first use wait-and-see, then, if needed, use reformation.

Why should this be so? In this setting, wait-and-see is a good first step:

- **Minimal Legal Friction.** There's no need to change the contingency or the document. It's just a matter of waiting. There's minimal legal friction.
- **Low Costs.** Costs are low. No court action is needed. It's just a matter of waiting and monitoring.
- **Contingencies Resolved.** As a practical matter, most contingencies are resolved within the wait-and-see period. It works.

Thus, after applying wait-and-see, many contingencies are resolved, and the Rule is satisfied. Much has already been sorted out, and with minimal cost.

Even after waiting, however, not all conditions may be resolved. Some still may be contingent. Most important, the end of the "wait" (and the perpetuities period) is approaching.

This is where reformation comes in. At this point, the extra price is paid, a reformation action is brought, and a final court-approved change is made.

2. The Final Plan—Combining Both Reforms

In summary, modern reform has two steps to validation.

Step One—Gray's Rule. If the contingency is valid under Gray's Rule—if there's a validating life—then nothing else is needed. It's immediately good.

Step Two—Fixing Errors. If an error is made, rather than striking it down (as Gray would do), there's a second way to validate:

- **Use Wait-and-See.** Here, watch if the contingency is "naturally" resolved by passage of time.
- **Reform the Contingency.** If the contingency still is not resolved near the end of the perpetuities period, then reform the contingency so it complies with Gray's Rule.

Once done, compliance with the Rule is guaranteed. One way or the other, it will be validated.

E. The Final Goal—Universal Compliance with the Rule

Modern reform for the Rule isn't about changing the Rule itself or abandoning its policies. Instead, it's about making compliance with the Rule universal. Using wait-and-see and reformation, together, can do that.

Here, modern reform turns sharply away from Gray. If a mistake is made, rather than striking it down—as Gray would do—a new question is asked: can we fix the lawyer's mistake so it follows the Rule?

Reform, here, celebrates the Rule. It values the policies of the Rule over human error. Most important, it helps lawyers use the Rule for their clients.

In the next chapter, we'll see how this works in modern statutory reform.

CHAPTER 17

The Age of Statutory Reform

Today, the law of Wills and Trusts is increasingly statutory.[1] Almost 20 states have adopted the Uniform Probate Code (UPC). And over 35 states have adopted the Uniform Trust Code. Much other uniform legislation—from the Uniform Prudent Investor Act to the Uniform Principal and Income Act—has been adopted as well.

The Rule against Perpetuities is another example. While grounded in Gray's Rule, perpetuities law today is largely statutory.

Here, two reforms dominate:

- **Uniform Statutory Rule Against Perpetuities (USRAP).** This is the dominant legislation. It starts with Gray's Rule, then uses wait-and-see plus reformation to fix mistakes.

- **Restatement (Third) of Property & Two Full Generations.** The most recent option is the "two-generation" proposal offered the American Law Institute (ALI). Instead of starting with Gray's Rule,

---

[1]   John Langbein, *Why Did Trust Law Become Statute Law in the United States?* 58 Ala. L. Rev. 1069 (2007).

it offers an alternative. It uses two full generations for the perpetuities period rather than the usual "life in being plus 21 years." Then, it uses wait-and-see along with reformation.

Let's take a look at each.

A. Uniform Statutory Rule Against Perpetuities— an Overview

First proposed in 1986, the Uniform Statutory Rule Against Perpetuities (USRAP[2]), is now the law in over half the states. The Uniform Statutory Rule also is part of the Uniform Probate Code (UPC §§ 2-901 to -906). Unlike some earlier piecemeal reforms, the Uniform Statutory Rule represents a total reform package.

USRAP has a two-step approach. First, the contingency is tested against Gray's Rule. If it's valid, USRAP upholds it. Nothing more is done.

If the contingency violates Gray's rule, however, it's not struck down. Instead, it's given a second chance at validation, using a full complement of reforms:

- Wait-and-See in the form of a uniform 90-year period.

- Reformation if wait-and-see doesn't resolve the contingency.

The goal: to cure any violations of the Rule. Alternatively, to make compliance with the Rule universal.

This keeps the basic policies of the Rule in place and furthers the intent of the donor. At the same time, it requires no new

---

[2] Pronunciation varies. Some say "use-rap," while others "us-rap." You can do either. See Ronald C. Link & Kimberly A. Licata, *Perpetuities Reform in North Carolina: The Uniform Statutory Rule against Perpetuities, Nondonative Transfers, and Honorary Trusts*, 74 North Carolina L. Rev. 1783, 1789 n.28 (1996).

learning by lawyers, reduces malpractice, and nearly eliminates perpetuities litigation.

1. The Validating Side of USRAP—Gray's Rule

The Uniform Statutory Rule starts with Gray's Rule. Drafters called this the *validating side* of the Uniform Statutory Rule. Under USRAP § 1(a)(1), an interest is valid if:

> [W]hen the interest is created, it is certain to vest or terminate no later than 21 years after the death of an individual then alive[.]

If this language sounds familiar, it should. It's Gray's Rule, pure and simple. All the key elements are there: contingencies, resolution, and lives in being plus 21 years. Thus, Gray's Rule hasn't been changed. It's just been put in slightly different language.[3]

The good news: here, no new learning is required. If a lawyer complies with Gray's Rule, nothing more is needed.

2. Invalidating Side of USRAP—90-Year Wait-and-See

The heart of USRAP reform is wait-and-see. Drafters called this the *invalidating side*. If a contingency violates Gray's Rule, it's not struck down. Instead, wait-and-see is applied. Significantly, the wait-and-see period is a uniform period of 90 years. USRAP § 1(a)(2).

3. Final USRAP Rule

Thus, once both sides are put together—both the validating and the invaliding side—the basic USRAP rule, § 1(a), reads like this:

---

[3] Why? Because all those law-review types can't help themselves. Let's keep them away from Lincoln's Gettysburg Address or Shakespeare's Sonnets.

(a) **[Validity of Nonvested Property Interest.]** A nonvested property interest is invalid unless:

(1) when the interest is created, it is certain to vest or terminate no later than 21 years after the death of an individual then alive; or

(2) the interest either vests or terminates within 90 years after its creation.

4. Wait-and-See as Statutory Saving Clause

For USRAP, the wait-and-see period of 90 years, with deferred reformation, operates as a statutory saving clause. In effect, it's similar to a traditional perpetuities saving clause. Here, though, USRAP offers a single statutory clause for all. This provides the same benefits typically given by an experienced drafter.

5. The 90-Year Uniform Period for Wait-and-See

In a general way, the 90-year period approximates what a typical "life in being plus 21 years" would be in practice. The uniform period also offers a consistent and easily applied standard.

For many classic traps, this offers a margin of safety. This allows an otherwise invalid contingency to work itself out naturally. If so, no reformation is needed. Most important, the donor's intent and contingency is upheld.

6. The Epic Scholarly Debate Behind the Scenes

Adopting a uniform 90-year period for wait-and-see was a small point for USRAP. But it was a big point for legal academics.

Behind the scenes, an epic scholarly debate played out. Jesse Dukeminier and Lawrence Waggoner—both wonderful scholars of the Rule—crossed academic swords. Each championed different wait-and-see standards. Professor Dukeminier argued for *causal lives*, basically persons connected to the contingency. In turn, Professor Waggoner argued a uniform period was easier and less complicated.

They debated, with full voice, in the law reviews. The main event was a five-article exchange in a single issue of the *Columbia Law Review*.[4] In the end, Waggoner won. USRAP used a uniform 90-year period.

7. Reformation Generally—USRAP § 3

If needed, reformation is an additional remedy. At the end of the 90-year period, if the contingency is not resolved, USRAP § 3 requires reformation. The preferred solution is insertion of a saving clause. USRAP § 5 Comment.

8. Reformation of Older Instruments—USRAP § 5(b)

USRAP is not retroactive. Significantly, however, it does enable reformation of earlier instruments. USRAP § 5(b). Thus, USRAP unambiguously gives courts the equitable power to reform instruments for violations of the Rule. The Comment to USRAP § 5(b) also makes clear that *Edgerly v. Barker*, 66 N.H. 434, 31 A. 900 (1891), the early reformation disdained so much by Gray, should be followed.

9. USRAP—a Few Fine Points

Charity-to-Charity Gifts. The traditional common-law exception for charity-to-charity gifts is preserved in USRAP § 4(5).[5]

---

[4] Jesse Dukeminier, *Perpetuities: The Measuring Lives*, 85 Colum. L. Rev. 1648 (1985); Lawrence Waggoner, *Perpetuities: A Perspective on Wait-and-See*, id. at 1714; Jesse Dukeminier, *A Response by Professor Dukeminier*, id. at 1730; Lawrence Waggoner, *A Rejoinder by Professor Waggoner*, id. at 1739; Jesse Dukeminier, *A Final Comment by Professor Dukeminier*, id. at 1742.

[5] See Chapter 14, at page 142.

Powers of Appointment—USRAP §§ 1(b), 1(c). The Uniform Statutory Rule has separate sections for powers of appointment. Following the traditional division for powers, one is for general powers. USRAP § 1(b). Another is for special and testamentary powers. USRAP § 1(c). The same two-step approach used for contingent property interests applies here as well.

Nondonative Transfers Outside the Family—USRAP § 4(1). From the *Duke of Norfolk's Case* forward, the Rule was centered on donative transfers within the family. Typically, this meant wills and trusts.

Some courts, however, applied the Rule to commercial transactions where title to land was made contingent. Examples include options for the purchase of land, rights of first refusal, and leases to commence in the future. Significantly, USRAP excludes commercial transactions from the Rule. USRAP § 4(1).

Two reasons are behind the change. First, the special measure of "lives in being" is best suited to family and generational gifts. Second, shorter periods may be best in commercial settings. For this reason, some states use special statutes for commercial transactions, often limiting the contingency period to several decades.[6]

Repeal of the Common-Law Rule—USRAP § 9. The common-law Rule against Perpetuities is repealed. USRAP § 9. Thus, the statute itself (and not Gray) becomes the source of the Rule.

---

[6] E.g., 765 Ill. Rev. Stat ch. 305, §§ 4(a)(5) (40 years for leases to begin in the future), 4(a)(7) (40 years for options in gross) (2017).

B. Restatement (Third) of Property—Two Full Generations

The most recent reform is the two-generation standard offered by the *Restatement (Third) of Property*. Significantly, it's unlike other reforms.

Earlier reforms, like USRAP, all started with Gray's Rule. If Gray's Rule was followed, nothing more was done. The Rule operated as it always had. But, if mistakes were made, reforms tried to fix them. The goal: make Gray's Rule work.

In contrast, *the Restatement (Third) of Property* goes a different way. It doesn't try to fix Gray's Rule, or even use it. Instead, it offers an alternative Rule.

Briefly, here's what the *Restatement* does:

- **Donative Gifts Within the Family.** It focuses on donative gifts within the family and, in particular, on trusts. This, of course, is almost the exclusive domain of the Rule today.

- **Two Younger Generations.** In that setting, it sets the perpetuities period as "two younger generations." The traditional "life in being plus 21 years" is gone. This dramatically simplifies the Rule.

- **Full Coverage of Grandchildren.** Unlike Gray's Rule, the Restatement covers all grandchildren. Significantly, this also includes grandchildren as yet unborn.

- **Perpetuities Period.** The perpetuities period is the collective lifetimes of the two generations. "However remote" isn't used. Instead, it's all about long the trust lasts.

- **Termination of Trusts.** At the end of two generations, the trust terminates. If needed, reformation is used.

This sounds simple (and it is).

Let's see how it works. And why it was needed.

1. What "Life in Being plus 21 Years" Did to Families

From the beginning, the Rule against Perpetuities was about families and generations. The *Duke of Norfolk's Case* only covered one generation.

It was limited to people then alive. Thus, if you knew the person (as the Earl of Arundel knew his eldest son), any contingency linked to them was valid.

Later, courts tacked on 21 more years. This added a second generation. But—and here is the key—it wasn't a full second generation. Instead, it stopped in between. In short, the common-law Rule splits the second generation.

Why does this matter? In truth, it was a not-so-minor addendum to Nottingham's rule. It didn't just add an extra 21 years. It also added a needless quirkiness to the Rule.

Gray thought the move to a free-floating 21 years was "highly convenient." But he also thought it was "arrived at by accident."[7] If so, it was one of the biggest accidents of the common law.

In the language of the Rule itself, the core concern was this: grandchildren alive on the effective date could be validating lives. But grandchildren born after the effective date couldn't.

---

[7]   John Chipman Gray, The Rule Against Perpetuities § 186, at 177 (4th ed. 1942).

In practice, this created all kinds of problems. It made the Rule more complicated than it had to be. It also created problems for families.

Let's see why.

2. Problems with Those Extra 21 Years—Equity Within the Same Generation

Under Gray's Rule, grandchildren born before the effective date got better treatment than grandchildren born after the effective date.

Living Grandchildren. Gifts to living grandchildren were easy. A donor could easily gift any living grandchild just by naming them. Most important, if linked to the named grandchild, any contingency could be used, too.

Why? Because the contingency would always be resolved within the life of the named grandchild. The named person always would be a validating life.

After-Born Grandchildren. In contrast, gifts to after-born grandchildren were limited. Here, the Rule allowed only a single contingency: reaching the age of 21. Anything else would violate the Rule.

In turn, this created two different classes of grandchildren inside the same generation. Each class had different rules. Plus, those born early got better treatment than those born late.

All this, it might be said, seemed a distant form of primogeniture. Benefits turned on birth order.

3. Problems with Those Extra 21 Years— Complications for Drafting

Having two classes made drafting difficult, too. Often, each needed different language.

Living Grandchildren vs. After-Born Grandchildren. A donor could use any contingency to help living grandchildren. But, with after-born grandchildren, only one condition was allowed: reaching the age of 21. Typically, this meant drafting different provisions for each.

Classic Traps. This lead to classic traps, too. One of the most famous: writing "grandchildren" when thinking (oh-so-reasonably) only of existing grandchildren. Once done, though, any contingency other than reaching 21 would violate the Rule.

4. Problems with Those Extra 21 Years—Donative Gifts & Families

From the start, the Rule focused on donative gifts within the family. And families, forever, cared about generations. Relationship by blood mattered, however thinned. Marriage mattered, too.

At the center, always, when it came to gifts at death was this question: who were children, grandchildren, and great-grandchildren? For donors, generations was the basic unit of giving.

But Gray's Rule drew the line across that thinking. Children got different treatment than grandchildren. And some grandchildren got different treatment than others. It didn't match the everyday thinking or practical needs of families.

5. Generations-Based Perpetuities—Another Option

But what if the Rule used a full second generation, instead?

That's, in essence, the idea behind the *Restatement (Third) of Property*. Instead of a life in being plus 21 years, it makes the perpetuity period *two younger generations.*

For the typical donor, this means two full generations—all their children and all their grandchildren. This gives a perpetuities period better tailored to how families typically think about generations and how trusts are used today.

6. *The* Restatement (Third)—an *Alternative Rule*

The *Restatement (Third) of Property* retains the basic policy of limiting dead-hand control along with periodic unencumbering of property. It also retains the basic measure of two generations.

The measure of two generations, however, is slightly altered. Measuring lives now include the donor and beneficiaries "no more than two generations younger." § 27.1(b)(1). In turn, the perpetuities period ends at the death of the last measuring life. So does the trust itself.

One additional twist. The *Restatement* doesn't prohibit gifts to even more distant beneficiaries, such as great grandchildren, if they are living and named. § 27.1(b)(2).[8]

7. *Wait-and-See & Reformation*

Here, the wait-and-see period is two full generations. At the death of the last measuring life, the trust ends. If it fails to end

---

[8] Once again, Nottingham's Rule.

before, a court can modify the trust. This ends the trust and requires final distribution of assets.

8. The End of Gray's Rule

Significantly, the *Restatement (Third) of Property* does something else, too: it abandons Gray's Rule. By using a two-generation wait-and-see standard, it leaves Gray's Rule and its messy technicalities behind.

Here, unlike USRAP, there's no two-step approach. The validating side of Gray's Rule is removed. Instead, it's all about wait-and-see and reformation.

As a result, note what no longer matters:

- Gray's Rule itself as a validating test.

- The distinction between contingent and vested interests.

- Classic traps like the Fertile Octogenarian.[9]

- The all-or-nothing rule for class gifts.

For law students, there's an added bonus: "The old learning under the common-law Rule that has perplexed generations of law students would be relegated to the dustbins of legal history."[10]

What would John Chipman Gray think? And what would Barton Leach think?

Ultimately, too, it's all consistent with the *Duke of Norfolk's Case.*

---

[9] Restatement (Third) of Property: Wills & Other Donative Transfers § 27.1, Reporter's Note, at 598 n.11 (describing common-law doctrines made obsolete) (2011).

[10] Lawrence W. Waggoner, *Congress Promotes Perpetual Trusts: Why?* 24 (2014), Law & Economics Working Papers, University of Michigan Law School, Paper 80.

9. Adoption of the Restatement Rule

What the *Restatement* does is simple and easy. At the same time, the *Restatement* proposal hasn't gotten the attention it deserves. Surprisingly, no state has yet adopted it. If anything, it's been underappreciated.

In part, though, it's because many states now have statutory versions of the Rule (such as USRAP). Many statutes, as part of their enactment, abolished the common-law Rule. As a result, courts have fewer options here than legislatures.

At the same time, the *Restatement (Third) of Property* offers a worthy model for future statutory reform. It's significant, too, it was drafted as a direct response to the "dynastic trust" movement.[11]

C. The Demise of Formalism—a New Age for Wills & Trusts as Well as Perpetuities

Today, formalism is on the wane, not only for perpetuities, but for wills and trusts as well. It's all about fixing mistakes. It's all, too, about a larger movement in modern estate planning.

In Gray's world, any mistake about perpetuities was fatal. Once an error was made, it could not be fixed. For lawyers, it was legal malpractice. For clients, it meant a lawyer's mistake trumped their own intent.

But this unforgiving formalism didn't apply just to mistakes about the Rule. Traditionally, the same approach applied to other mistakes lawyers made in drafting wills, too.

---

[11] See Chapter 18, at 193.

Here's a sampling:

- **Drafting Mistakes About Other Gifts in the Will.**
  Mistakes about other gifts in a will could not be fixed
  either. Here, a similar "no reformation" rule applied
  to wills generally.[12]

- **Mistakes About Execution of the Will.** Mistakes
  about the formalities of executing wills were fatal,
  too. Again, the intent of the testator didn't
  matter.[13]

The common theme for such mistakes—all similar to those
about the Rule—was this: if a lawyer made a mistake, you couldn't
fix the will.

In recent decades, though, reforms for wills paralleled those
for perpetuities. On the one hand, reformation and wait-and-see
fixed mistakes about the Rule. On the other hand, harmless error[14]
and full reformation[15] fixed other mistakes about executing or
drafting wills.

All were reactions to formalism. All, too, centered on elevating
donor intent.

Together, these reforms for wills have similar goals to those
for the Rule:

- Enforce the known intent of the donor.

- Prevent malpractice and reduce litigation.

---

[12] E.g., Mahoney v. Grainger, 186 N.E. 86, 87 (Mass. 1933) (mistake by lawyer in describing intended beneficiaries of will).

[13] E.g., In re Groffman, [1969] 1 W.L.R. 733 (PC) (witnesses not "in presence of" each other because cumbrous friend slow getting into room).

[14] Uniform Probate Code § 2-503 (2010); Restatement (Third) of Property: Wills & Other Donative Transfers § 3.3 (1999).

[15] Uniform Probate Code § 2-805 (2010). Similar rules exist for trusts. See Uniform Trust Code § 415 (2010).

- Avoid unjust enrichment by disappointed heirs who profit—at the expense of the donor's intended beneficiaries—by raising technical mistakes by lawyers.

Thus, recent reforms for wills are similar to those for the Rule. They go together.

PART 6

The Future & Policies
of the Rule

Congress, Taxes, & Abolition of the Rule— the Humpty-Dumpty World of Modern Perpetuities

A. Didn't They Just Abolish That?

There's talk today of abolishing the Rule, and some states have. But the modern abolition movement has nothing to do with the merits of the Rule. Instead, it's all about avoiding taxes. How did this happen?

1. The Inadvertent Role of the Generation-Skipping Tax

It all started simple enough. Here are the pieces:

- In 1986 Congress enacted a generation-skipping tax (GST) to close a loophole in the estate tax when property passed from one generation to another.[1]

---

[1]   I.R.C. §§ 2601–2663 (2021).

- But there was an important *exemption* for the GST tax if the trust was under $5 million.[2]

- Nested inside all this taxing was a simple assumption: the Rule against Perpetuities, a creature of the states, would limit the duration of GST-exempt trusts.

What could possibly go wrong?

2. *The South Dakota Ad*

Then, from the states, came a move Congress never anticipated. And it changed the game.

It started with South Dakota. Imagine a glossy print ad, stamped with the logo of a major bank.[3] Then, against a quiet pastoral scene of a barn and crops, is the following language, all in bold:

> You don't have to live in South Dakota to benefit from a South Dakota Legacy Trust

Then comes the pitch any law student would love:

> Imagine a place where there is no rule against perpetuities. Where there is no fiduciary income tax. And where a knowledgeable, experienced staff can make a generation skipping trust possible.

The message is clear: bring your trusts and your money here. Why? Because we abolished the Rule against Perpetuities. Come here and your taxes on GST-exempt trusts will never come due.

---

[2] I.R.C. §§ 2631(c), 2010(c) (2021). As of 2021, it's now $11.7 million for individuals and twice that for married couples.

[3] A picture of the ad can be found in Robert H. Sitkoff & Jesse Dukeminier, Wills, Trusts, & Estates 908 (10th ed. 2017).

3. The State vs. State Battle for Dynastic Trusts & Fees

Then came the flood: a competition for trust business—state vs. state—with over half the states either abolishing the Rule or extending it well beyond two generations.

The *dynastic trust* had arrived. Here's the basic package:

- **Abolish or Drastically Extend the Rule.** Enact laws favoring GST-exempt trusts. This means either abolishing the Rule entirely or extending it to long periods, such as 350 or even 1000 years.

- **Conflict of Laws.** Advertise a basic point of modern trust law—choice of law. For trusts of personal property—which means almost all modern wealth— the settlor can pick the situs or location of the trust.[4]

- **In-State Management.** Require management by an in-state bank or trust company. This is the key provision. With it comes long-term management and, as important, long-term fees.

In practice, it rivals the technicalities and powers of medieval conveyancing. And it's every bit as lucrative.

4. Did It Work?

Did it work? For some states, remarkably well. A leading study estimated about $100 billion in trust assets flowed to states allowing dynastic trusts.[5] And, basic math also suggests, about $1 billion every year in fees.

---

4 Uniform Trust Code §§ 107(1), 108 (2010).
5 Robert H. Sitkoff & Max M. Schanzenbach, *Jurisdictional Competition for Trust Funds: An Empirical Analysis of Perpetuities and Taxes* 115 Yale L.J. 356, 412–14 (2005).

But the key point was this: abolition had nothing to do with the merits of the Rule. Instead, it was about avoiding taxes.[6] Thus, "abolition of the Rule is pure serendipity."[7]

B. The Modern Battle Lines

Thus, the modern battle lines are drawn.

On the one side are large trust companies and banks, and sophisticated estate planners. They wrote and got enacted statutes to abolish or limit the Rule. Their clear goal: use the loophole left by Congress to help moneyed clients avoid taxes. The states gaining trust business and fees are happy, too.

On the other side are many academics and the American Law Institute. The *Restatement (Third) of Property* was the first significant perpetuities reform after the rise of dynastic trusts. The ALI urged a fix by Congress and offered an elegant and updated full two-generation version of the Rule.[8]

At the same time, the ALI also took a strong public stance against the dynastic trust movement, labeling it "ill advised" policy:

> It is the considered judgment of The American Law Institute that the recent statutory movement allowing the creation of perpetual or multiple-centuries trusts is ill advised.[9]

It wasn't just a passing thought, either. The ALI backed its statement with 17 pages of small-print argument.[10]

---

[6] Max M. Schanzenbach & Robert H Sitkoff, *Perpetuities or Taxes? Explaining the Rise of the Perpetual Trust*, 27 Cardozo L. Rev. 2465, 2496–98 (2006).

[7] Jesse Dukeminier & James Krier, *The Rise of the Perpetual Trust*, 50 UCLA L. Rev. 1303, 1317 (2003).

[8] Restatement (Third) of Property: Wills & Other Donative Transfers § 27.1 (2011).

[9] Id. Chapter 27, Introductory Note 564.

[10] Id. at 554-71.

C. The Role of Congress—Politics & Taxes

In the middle sits Congress. Because of the GST debacle, "Congress has come to be in charge of trust duration."[11]

Predictions about taxes and politics always are difficult. But three options seem likely:

- **The Status Quo.** If Congress does nothing, dynastic trusts continue with its blessing. And the federal government continues to lose tax revenues.

- **A Fix by Congress.** Congress could fix the loophole. One option: force states to bring back the Rule. This could be done by limiting the GST exemption to a standard perpetuities period. One proposal, offered by the Reporter for the *Restatement (Third) of Property*, would let states pick from three options: the common law version (as endorsed by USRAP); the USRAP 90-year wait-and-see; or the two-generation period of the *Restatement*.[12] Any of these, in turn, would revive the exemption. This also would promote debate on updating the Rule.

- **Repeal of the Estate Tax.** If the estate tax is abolished, the situation gets interesting. The loophole behind dynastic trusts goes away. If so, would abolition, once done, stay in place? If not, who would lobby to get the Rule back? Among other things, it could spur on a debate between the two modern statutory reforms, USRAP and the *Restatement (Third) of Property*.

---

[11] Jesse Dukeminier & James Krier, supra note 7, at 1343.

[12] Lawrence W. Waggoner, *Congress Promotes Perpetual Trusts: Why?* 34-36 (2014), Law & Economics Working Papers, University of Michigan Law School, Paper 80.

D. The Future

These are exciting times for the Rule against Perpetuities. One way or another, the debate will come. And you get to be part of it.

Thus, the next chapter sets out some big ideas about the Rule. It's something you'll need to know.

A Few Big Ideas—
the Policies Behind
the Rule

A. A Few Big Ideas

Law often is about a few big ideas. The Rule against Perpetuities is no different. Often lost in the hard-spun and tangled details of the Rule, is the larger role it plays in daily life.

In all, four reasons traditionally are offered for the Rule:

- **Alienability of Real Property.** The Rule keeps property in circulation and aids commerce.

- **Limiting Dead-Hand Control.** The Rule balances, fairly, the ownership of resources between generations.

- **Practical Matters of Trusts.** The Rule serves as a balance point for the work of trusts.

- **Limiting Hereditary Wealth.** The Rule limits long-term protection of hereditary wealth.

Once done, it's easier to assess both the modern Rule and the debate about dynastic trusts.

After 350 years, we can see this: the role of the Rule has changed over time. The original role it played in promoting alienability of real property is less important today. At the same time, the Rule still plays an important role in American law.

B. Policy # 1—Real Property & Alienability

The argument longest tied to the Rule is alienability. As John Chipman Gray argued over a century ago, the Rule helps keep property in circulation:

> The system of rules disallowing restrains on alienation and the Rule against Perpetuities are the two modes adopted by the Common Law for forwarding the circulation of property which it is its policy to promote.[1]

This matters more for real property than personal property, and more for deeds than trusts.

1. The Big Picture of Real Property

For use, real property is often divided into pieces. For example, you might have any of the following:

- Multiple owners of a single piece (e.g., joint tenancy).

- Multiple pieces at a single time (e.g., surface vs. mineral interests).

- Different owners of a single piece over time (e.g., future interests).

---

[1]   John Chipman Gray, The Rule Against Perpetuities § 2.1, at 4 (4th ed. 1942).

All of this is good. But society also gains if, periodically, all pieces move back together into single, clean title. Once done, this promotes growth and innovation.[2]

Different property rules help, in different ways, to aid alienability. This includes such varied things as the self-healing of joint tenancies after death of a party, the limiting of time for rights of entry,[3] and the reassembly of property by marketable title acts.[4]

What role, in turn, does the Rule play in matters of alienability? And is it still valid today?

2. Contingent Title in Real Property—for Future Interests in Donees

Historically, this is where the Rule mattered most. If legal title is contingent, there's little market for it. Typically, this involves contingent remainders and executory interests.

Here's an example, similar to the *Duke of Norfolk's Case*:

The Farm to A, but if B dies without issue during the life of A, then to C.

During the life of B, title to Farm is contingent. A owns Farm, but title might shift later to C. It all depends on what happens to another person, B.

While title is contingent, it's unmarketable. Why? No one would buy it. Neither A nor C has much to sell. What A has, A may not keep. And what C wants, C may not get. Plus, no buyer could predict when possession might come.

---

[2] Jeffrey Evans Stake, *Darwin, Donations, and the Illusion of Dead Hand Control*, 64 Tulane L. Rev. 705, 716-20 (1990).

[3] E.g., Mass. Gen. Laws ch. 184A § 7 (2017) (30 years). Other states require recording to preserve rights of entry or possibility of reverter. Minn. Stat. § 541.023 (2016) (40 years).

[4] Uniform Marketable Title Act § 3 (1990) (30 years).

In turn, A has little incentive to invest. Why? A may lose ownership, years later and A can't do anything to control it. Everything depends on the life of another person, B. Until the contingency's resolved, A may limit investment.

Thus, "the value of the present interest *plus* the value of the executory gift will fall far short of what would be the value of the property if there were no executory interest."[5] As a result, contingent title limits alienability and deters investment. If so, commerce and industry slow. By limiting how long contingent title is allowed, therefore, the Rule helps keep property marketable.

3. The Mitigating Role of Trusts & Personal Property

Contingent title matters most for real property. Today, though, this is rare. Except for the rare deed or will drafted by a layperson, virtually all future interests are in trust.

There's a reason. The trustee holds single legal title. Trusts thus maintain control over several generations, but mitigate problems of alienability and control. Plus, entire family groups can be named as beneficiaries.

Most important, almost all property in trust today is personal property. Rather than the immovable landed estates of old, it's now the liquid wealth of bonds, stocks, and cash. Thus, in practice, the application of the Rule to real property today is limited.

---

[5] This quote may sound like Judge Richard Posner, but it's really John Chipman Gray. See John Chapman Gray, The Rule Against Perpetuities § 268, at 297 (4th ed. 1942) (emphasis in original). Law & Economics is older than you think.

C. Policy # 2—Generation vs. Generation— Dead Hands & Others

Property scholar Lewis Simes is often cited as saying the Rule strikes a balance between generations:

[T]he Rule against Perpetuities strikes a fair balance between the desires of members of the present generation, and similar desires of succeeding generations, to do what they wish with the property which they enjoy.[6]

What does this really mean? How far into the future can a generation control property? And are later generations duty-bound to accept it?

1. *Dead Hands & Others*

Here, there are battling arguments. It's all about justice between generations.

On the one hand, a classic argument for limiting control by earlier generations is the *dead hand* of the past. It's a cold image. Once a person has died, they argue, why should they still control property? The dead cannot see and they cannot know. The living know better. The longer the time, too, the worse it gets. Once frozen in time, it haunts the living.

On the other hand, gifts in the family have competing images. Instead of the dead hand, it's the warm and caring hands of parents. Parents want to care for children and grandchildren. Parents want to protect them, too, even after their own lives have ended. They also want to preserve family wealth. To do that, parents may look to trusts and contingencies to control gifts for the future.

---

[6] Lewis M. Simes, *The Policy Against Perpetuities*, 103 U. Pa. L. Rev. 707, 723 (1955).

When does a caring hand become something else unwanted? Arguably, it's a matter of generations.

2. Generation vs. Generation—Rolling Sets of Reciprocal Arrangements

The basic bargain is this. The first generation controls for a time. Once done, the pieces of property go back together and title is clear. At that point, a later generation can do it all over again.

Later generations accept what earlier ones do because they, in turn, want to do it, too. Thus, while the current generation may be bound, in some areas, by gifts from the past generation, it also gets to bind, in other areas, gifts to the next generation. All in all, there's a rolling set of reciprocal arrangements.

Each generation gets its turn. As some controls expire, others start up, continually updating at each new turn of the generational wheel. Overall, it takes the form of generational reciprocity. If it works, both generations are better off.

3. Different Periods for Different Purposes

But how long should the period be? It's easy to imagine different periods for different needs.

For example, shorter limits may be best for commercial or business property, reflecting a shorter business cycle. Thus, several decades are often used for marketable title acts or limitations on rights of entry.

On the other hand, longer limits—even perpetuities—may be best for charities because of broad and lasting public benefit.

For donative transfers within the family, in turn, it may be something in-between. Here, Nottingham may have had it right: it's about people you know. The best measure may be how it's done in families—by generations.

And, here, *two generations* may be about right. For donors, this measures, in a general way, how many generations next you know in life. For parents, it's children and grandchildren. At the other end, two generations in life is when living descendants typically last know the donor. As long as a living connection remains, they're joined. That makes basic human sense. Thus, "[a] clear, obvious, natural line is drawn for us between those persons and events which the Settlor knows and sees, and those which [the Settler] cannot know or see."[7]

4.   The Problematics of Dynastic Trusts

Once more than two generations past, the tables turn. The living human connection is gone. Why should donors get to control people they'll never know? Why should donors get to control people in the future, all as yet unborn?

Why, in turn, should beneficiaries accept control from a person who never saw their face? Why should a person, now long gone, rule over the living?

When we go four or five generations, or even all generations future, it arguably becomes caprice, ego, or whim. If you want to be remembered that long, it could be said, then endow a school, a professorship, or a park. Charities are forever.

Two generations is about right.

D. Policy # 3—Property Reboots & Practical Problems of Trusts

In operation, the Rule forces periodic reassembly of property. Every two generations, property—once in separate pieces—goes back together. Contingencies are resolved, beneficiaries are known,

---

[7]   Arthur Hobhouse, *The Devolution and Transfer of Land*, in The Dead Hand: Addresses on the Subject of Endowments and Settlements of Property 168, 188 (1880).

and alienability again is full. Going forward, property now can be put to new use. If needed, it can be divided, once again, in new ways. In modern terms, it reboots.

1. Trusts & Reboots—the Rule as Proxy for Practical Matters for Trusts

But the same reboot also applies to trusts. And, here, it matters more. Since the Rule also limits the length of trusts, a parallel reboot applies. After two generations, a new trust must be made. Assets must be gathered, beneficiaries named, and provisions drafted. Thus, the Rule forces regular legal updates.

The Rule as Proxy for Foreseeability. As a practical matter, the two-generation limit confines the trust to a limited forward time. While rough, the Rule serves as reasonably proxy for general matters of foreseeability. For practical matters of trusts, in other words, the two-generation limit does not seem arbitrary.

The Rule as a Limit on the Number of Beneficiaries. As applied, the Rule also confines trusts to a limited and largely known number of beneficiaries. The number of children and grandchildren, even for large families, will be limited.

Beyond two generations, this changes drastically. After two generations, each new generation brings geometric growth. For example, if we assume 25 years per generation with each having 2 births, here's what we get, overtime, for numbers of beneficiaries:

- At 100 years = 64 descendants.

- At 200 years = 1,024 descendants.

- At 300 years = 16,384 descendants.

- At 400 years = 262,144 descendants.[8]

---

[8]　3 Restatement (Third) of Property: Wills & Other Donative Transfers, Chapter 27, Introductory Note 557-58 (2011) (table for generations 1 to 20).

Thus, trusts for three or four generations are much different from trusts for two. Perpetual trusts, by definition, are exponentially so.

2. Upsetting the Equipoise of Trusts—the Limits of Form

Basic trust law assumes the Rule in place and working. The two go together. The Rule limits the length of trusts. In turn, basic trust law assumes two generations of beneficiaries as the norm. Thus, basic trust law is not designed for perpetual trusts. Neither is the basic trust form.

Even inside two generations, flexibility matters. New or unseen events may require adjustments. Here, such things as powers of appointment and trust doctrines like equitable deviation can mitigate some problems.[9] At the same time, exponential growth in beneficiaries can't as easily be remedied. Neither can centuries of change.

As such, trusts longer than two generations are not a plus. Overall, periodic rebooting does it better. If longer control and family ownership matter, then other legal forms like private corporations or charities may be better.

E. Policy # 4—Protected Hereditary Wealth— Fee Tails in America

1. The New Fee Tail

The fee tail estate is not recognized in American Law.

> —Restatement (Third) of Property: Wills & Other Donative Transfers § 24.4 (2011)

---

[9] Uniform Trust Code § 412 (2010).

Once the Rule against Perpetuities is abolished, a new form of the *fee tail* returns.[10] For dynastic trusts, this the heart of the debate. What worth is the revival of this old form today and, in particular, what political ghosts come with it? Should fee tails be allowed again or not?

To understand the issue, it's first important to see how the Rule works to limit dynastic trusts. Then you can better appreciate why a dynastic trust brings back the fee tail.

2. How the Rule Limits the Life Cycle of Protected Family Wealth

With the Rule in place, the typical family trust runs through a predictable, two-generation lifecycle:

- **Two Generations.** Once created, the trust exists for no longer than two generations.

- **Wealth Stays Within the Family.** During that time, the wealth stays within the family, managed by the trustee. The property itself thus maintains a family identity.

- **Spendthrift Protection for Beneficiaries.** Today, virtually every private trust contains a spendthrift clause. This makes the beneficiary's interest *inalienable*. In effect, it creates a right in property the beneficiary cannot offer for security and which most creditors cannot take for debt.[11]

- **Spendthrift Protection for Family Wealth.** The spendthrift clause also keeps family wealth intact.

---

[10] Jeffery Evans Stake, *Evolution of Rules in a Common Law System: Differential Litigation of the Fee Tail and Other Perpetuities*, 32 Fla. St. L. Rev. 401, 421-23 (2005).

[11] Uniform Trust Code § 502 (2010); Restatement (Third) of Trusts § 58(1) (2003).

Why? The beneficiary can't put the corpus of the trust at risk. Family wealth is protected.

At the end of two generations, however, everything resets. This means a fresh start, a new mix of ownership, and unencumbered assets:

- **Reset.** The trust is terminated. The property—now fully alienable—is distributed to the beneficiaries. In turn, the beneficiaries, looking forward, have full use. They can spend, risk, or invest. Also, if so disposed, they can create new two-generation trusts for their own children and grandchildren.

- **Termination of Protected Status—Beneficiaries.** The protected status stops. Beneficiaries now have full and unencumbered title. They can alienate the property. They can risk it all, as well. Ordinary rules for creditors apply, too. If beneficiaries wanted, they could then set up new trusts for their own families.

- **Termination of Protected Status—Family Wealth.** Family wealth no longer has protected status. Rather than being held in trust, for the family, it's now split and owned, individually, by the beneficiaries. Management shifts from perpetual trustees back to living beneficiaries.

3. *The Different Life Cycle for Dynastic Trusts*

In the world of dynastic trusts, the cycle changes significantly. Most important, control stays centralized and wealth stays protected:

- **No Reset.** The trust continues, generation after generation, as a series of life estates. There is no reset.

- **Extended Trustee Control.** Trustees and trust companies continue management indefinitely. Control is not returned to beneficiaries within two generations.

- **Long-Term Protection of Beneficiaries.** Spendthrift protection and inalienability continue indefinitely. Later beneficiaries can't encumber or sell assets.

- **Long-Term Consolidation of Family Wealth.** Consolidated family wealth, with centralized control, continues as single unit. Family wealth is safe from alienation or risk by beneficiaries.

4. Dynastic Trusts—Two Sides of Alienability

A basic feature of a trust is this: it splits ownership. The trustee holds *legal* title, while the beneficiary holds *equitable* title.

When it comes to alienability, therefore, dynastic trusts have two very different sides. On the trustee's side, the legal interest is *alienable*. Today, most trusts are personal property and the trustee has the power of sale. The property of the trust can be bought and sold.

But with the dynastic trusts, there's an *inalienable* side, too—the beneficiary's equitable interest. Here, the interest itself cannot be sold. It stays, life interest after life interest, in the family. And it stays, at each stage, protected.

Thus, much like the fee tail in real property from centuries ago, each successive beneficiary's interest is unbarrable—it is held "indefinitely in the family secure . . . from creditors or improvident disposition."[12]

5. The Rule & Equitable Interests in Trusts

The Rule against Perpetuities applies to equitable interests in trusts, even if the trustee has power of sale and the property, itself, is alienable. The point was firm in Gray's treatise:

> The Rule applies not only to interests in particular pieces of property, but also to interests in changeable funds. The interests of *cestuis que trust* may be too remote, although the trustees have full power to change investments.[13]

The rationale: it prevents the remote beneficiary's interest from being used for a beneficiary's immediate needs or invested anew in other ways. It's all about tying up assets. Even if no specific property is made inalienable, a perpetuity still exists if the assets of the trust can only be applied in one way forever.

As explained in the *Restatement (Second) of Property*, it's a matter of limiting the ultimate use of the property:

> [The Rule's] function has broadened to include the prevention of limitations which "freeze" or "tie up" property for too long, even though no specific thing has been made inalienable, even for a moment.[14]

Here, later beneficiaries would never be allowed to invest or risk the property. It would remain in a trust account, locked forever.

Thus, while putting property in trust helps markets in some ways, it also allows dynasties and reinforces disparate treatment of

---

[12] Herbert Barry, *The Duke of Norfolk's Case*, 23 Va. L. Rev. 538, 539 (1937) (describing the fee tail).

[13] John Chipman Gray, The Rule Against Perpetuities § 202.1, at 193 (4th ed. 1942). A similar point is made in § 269, at 298-99.

[14] Restatement (Second) of Property, The Rule Against Perpetuities and Related Rules as Applied to Donative Transfers 10 (1983).

families. Property is kept in the same family, regardless of whether the trustee can sell.

6. The New Equitable Fee Tail

As the *Restatement (Third) of Property* has recognized, dynastic trusts create the substantial equivalent of successive life estates in income. As a result, dynastic trusts create an *equitable fee tail*.[15]

Here's how a dynastic trust operates as an equitable fee tail:

- The moneyed estate itself remains intact and undiminished.

- The life tenant (beneficiary) is disabled from alienating her present interest.

- The process continues, generation after generation, so long as heirs remain.

- The choice is made by the original generation. Once done, it can't be altered.

- All of this is authorized and furthered by law.

Thus, dynastic trusts allow wealth to be locked up in the family by law. Each successive generation has guaranteed hereditary wealth.

In legal terms, the question for dynastic trusts is simply this: should fee tails be allowed in trusts and, if so, for how long?

---

[15] Restatement (Third) of Property: Wills & Other Donative Transfers § 24.4, cmt. c, at 438 (2011).

7. Political Ghosts—Social Aspects of Perpetuities

Perpetuities . . . are contrary to the genius of a free state and shall not be allowed.

—North Carolina Constitution, Art. 1, § 34

Perpetuities are not favored in America. For many, the word *perpetuity* evokes images of an old and inegalitarian world. It's a world filled with lasting social rank, hereditary privilege, and landed elites. With the American Revolution, the world here was thought born anew.

In response, some states passed statutes about entails. But other states wanted even stronger statements. Foremost were concerns about dynastic concentrations of wealth. For some states, it took on a matter of deep political principle. Today, eleven states have constitutional prohibitions on perpetuities. In such states, dynastic trusts, are constitutionally suspect.[16]

Dynastic trusts are troublesome in another and more general way, too—basic American politics. It wasn't just fee tails or banning titles of nobility.[17] It was bigger than that: it was that nobility, in any legal form, was gone. For them, letting wealthy families control property for "too long" wasn't just an economic wrong to markets. Instead, it was something more—it was a political wrong, too.

As expressed at the time, it was that people, families, and generations stood on their own. That whatever was left of the fee tail elsewhere, symbolic or otherwise, even less was welcome here:

[Entailments have] no application to republican establishments, where wealth does not form a permanent distinction . . . Every family, stripped of artificial

---

[16] This is well covered in Steven J. Horowitz & Robert H. Sitkoff, *Unconstitutional Perpetual Trusts*, 67 Vanderbilt L. Rev. 1769 (2011).

[17] U.S. Const. art I, § 9 ("No Title of Nobility shall be granted by the United States.").

supports, is obliged, in this country, to repose upon the virtue of its descendants for the perpetuity of its fame.[18]

Set against this egalitarian ethic, guaranteed hereditary wealth or privilege—through the generations—was suspect. Here, the modern dynastic trust invites comparisons. Wealth is one thing. Wealth endowed by law with hereditary power, it could be said, is another. The core fault of the fee tail remains unchanged: letting wealthy families control property for "too long" is politically wrong. That applies as much to stocks and bonds as it does to land.

8. *Some Quintessential American Questions*

Beneficiaries of spendthrift trusts get protection from most creditors. It's also protection wage-earners and entrepreneurs don't get. Dynastic trusts with spendthrift protection continue this forever.

Put blunt, the political rub is this: should hereditary wealth get protection wages and daily earnings don't? In short, do such dynastic trusts raise what could be called matters of equal protection writ large?

Here are some quintessential American questions:

- Should families have the right, in perpetuity, to protect members from common birth?

- Does hereditary protection from creditors and ill-fortune raise questions about equality of treatment for others, not so born, the same day?

- What is the social worth in extending guaranteed wealth to generations beyond those the donor knew?

---

[18]   James Kent, 4 Commentaries on American Law *20 (O.W. Holmes ed. 12th ed. 1873).

- Does this raise a larger matter of *permanent* class and privilege distinct from other American families?

Who said the Rule against Perpetuities was boring?

PART 7

A Final Look at the Rule

CHAPTER 20

What Would Nottingham Say?

These are exciting times for the Rule against Perpetuities, perhaps the most exciting in 350 years. There's serious talk about the policies behind the Rule. And there's talk, too, of what the future of the Rule may be.

What final lessons does this have for law students? What is the future of the Rule?

A. Unraveling the Mystery of the Rule

The Rule, once explained, is not the deep mystery it's so often made to be. It's not about math or strange worlds. Instead, it's about families, death, and control of property by generations.

This much, too, is true: in a world of only fee tails or only fee simples, there's no need for the Rule. Markets or families would take care of everything.

Only after the common law created multi-generational property, like future interests, was the Rule was needed. And then, too, only after families added conditions. Once conditions were joined with future interests, it put families against markets in a new way. And the Rule, in its balance, gave a new answer.

Ultimately, the *Duke of Norfolk's Case* was a concession to families. Nottingham allowed families—for a time—to keep property inalienable to provide for family contingencies "in immediate prospect."[1] Once done, the Rule allowed families to plan for different futures. And for that limited time, families could keep property and wealth protected.

The price for this control was limiting gifts and trusts to two generations. Past that, the Rule required clear title and repurposing of property. The reason: to avoid family dynasties sanctioned by law.

Over the last 350 years, none of this has changed. While wealth has moved from real estate to liquid funds, families and society still have the same needs and interests. And markets still function as markets.

B. The Modern Rule

The Rule need not be complicated. Even with Gray's rule, the mistakes tend to fall into classic categories. Many, too, are easily fixed. Two generations is not so difficult.

Today, with modern reforms, the good news is this: the Rule can be enforced without being fatal. Gone are the days when the Rule destroyed property and disregarded intent.

C. Future Options

Where does the Rule go from here? Some states have abolished the Rule. But everyone agrees it's about avoiding taxes, not the merits of the Rule itself. It's hard to imagine it willfully done.

---

[1]   Duke of Norfolk's Case, 22 Eng. Rep. 931, 955 (Ch. 1682).

Whatever happens to the federal tax loophole, more debate about the Rule seems certain. And then it happens, some larger questions are likely. One is the choice between the Uniform Statutory Rule Against Perpetuities (USRAP) and the new, full two-generation model of the *Restatement (Third) of Property.*

Today, the dominant statutory form of the Rule is the Uniform Statutory Rule Against Perpetuities (USRAP). Gray's Rule remains intact, but wait-and-see and reformation cure any violations. So done, it offers universal compliance with the Rule.

In contrast, the *Restatement (Third) of Property* gives the Rule a change of heart. Unlike Gray's Rule, it's not about the remoteness of vesting. Instead, it's about donative transfers within the family and limiting dead-hand control. By using wait-and-see and reformation, it limits trusts to two full generations. Most important, it offers a simple and elegant version of the Rule. It's one more attuned to the natural interests of families. And one, too, far easier to learn, apply, and defend.

Thus, one modern option starts with Gray's Rule, while the other abandons it. But both are consistent with what Nottingham said, centuries before, in the *Duke of Norfolk's Case.*

D. The Future of the American Fee Tail—Big Questions of Property

The problem of perpetuities is not a passing one. It's always been about families, wealth, and generations. In one form or the other, it's been the same question for over 800 years: how long do families, as families, get to control wealth? The stages are well known to students of Property:

Stage One—1285 to 1472—the Fee Tail. In 1285, fee tails were permitted by statute. Fee tail estates kept land in the family generation after generation, as a perpetual series of life estates.

Response: fee tails were abolished by common recovery, giving the life tenant a fee simple. Each generation then had full alienability.

Stage Two—1472 to 1682—Development of Future Interests. In response, lawyers created future interests. By splitting property into pieces over time, families could control property over multiple generations. Then, families tried to control even more with contingent remainders, which raised issues of contingent title. **Response:** destruction of contingent remainders and the Rule in Shelley's Case.

Stage Three—1682 to Present—Executory Interests & the Rule Against Perpetuities. The Statute of Uses (1536) allowed executory interests, another form of contingent title. Then executory interests were found nondestructible. Once again, there was hint of new fee tails. **Response:** *Duke of Norfolk's Case* (1682) and the Rule against Perpetuities ultimately limited control to two generations.

Where, then, do we go from here?

Today, the argument is a big one: some states have brought back an equitable fee tail in the form of dynastic trusts. Once again, the issue is surrounded by strong personalities, strong politics, and the swirl of wealth. And, once again, it's raising big questions about families, property, and control of wealth in perpetuity.

The perpetuity so feared in the *Duke of Norfolk's Case* now, in some places, is back.

What would Nottingham say? And, most important, what would he do?